The Bible

How do we know it can be trusted?

WHY 66? • IS THE BIBLE ENOUGH? • BIBLE CONTRADICTIONS • THE TRUTH OF SCRIPTURE • OTHER RELIGIOUS WRITINGS • CREATION: WHERE'S THE PROOF? • WHAT IS A BIBLICAL WORLD VIEW?

A POCKET GUIDE TO . . .

The Bible

How do we know it can be trusted?

1:1
answersingenesis
Petersburg, Kentucky, USA

Sixth printing: February 2012

ISBN: 1-60092-265-1

Printed in China

www.answersingenesis.org

Table of Contents

Introduction

There are many different religions, each with their own religious writings. What makes the Bible any different from the rest? The answer to this question is extremely important. If you don't know the answer, the articles presented in this book will help you understand what sets the Bible apart. More than just a book that gives us good moral guidance, the Bible claims to contain the very words of God—the Creator of the universe.

If the Bible is truly God's Word, then we should take it seriously. For thousands of years, this book has been reverenced by millions of people as the only source of truth. These people have found the answers to the origin of the universe, the meaning of life, and what comes after we die. The Bible provides consistent, reasonable answers from the very God of the universe. We can put our trust in it.

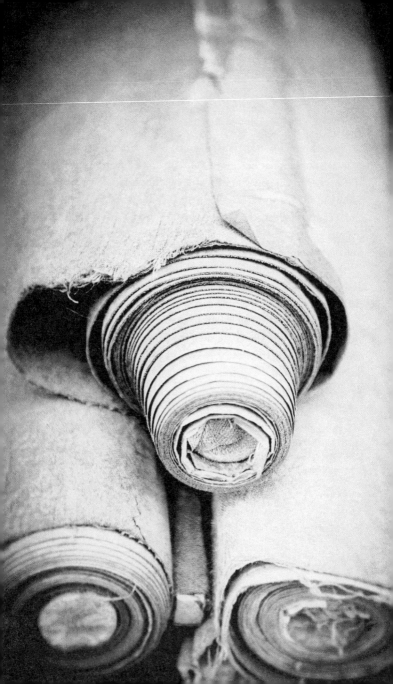

Why 66?

by Brian H. Edwards

How can we be sure that we have the correct 66 books in our Bible? The Bible is a unique volume. It is composed of 66 books by 40 different writers over 1,500 years. But what makes it unique is that it has one consistent story line running all the way through, and it has just one ultimate author—God. The story is about God's plan to rescue men and women from the devastating results of the Fall, a plan that was conceived in eternity, revealed through the prophets, and carried out by the Son of God, Jesus Christ.

Each writer of the Bible books wrote in his own language and style, using his own mind, and in some cases research, yet each was so overruled by the Holy Spirit that error was not allowed to creep into his work. For this reason, the Bible is understood by Christians to be a book without error.[1]

This collection of 66 books is known as the "canon" of Scripture. That word comes from the Hebrew *kaneh* (a rod), and the Greek *kanon* (a reed). Among other things, the words referred equally to the measuring rod of the carpenter and the ruler of the scribe. It became a common word for anything that was the measure by which others were to be judged (see Galatians 6:16, for example). After the apostles, church leaders used it to refer to the body of Christian doctrine accepted by the churches. Clement and Origen of Alexandria, in the third century, were possibly the first to employ the word to refer to the Scriptures (the Old Testament).[2] From then on, it became more common in Christian use with reference to a collection of books that are fixed in their number, divine in their origin, and universal in their authority.

In the earliest centuries, there was little *debate* among Christians over which books belonged in the Bible; certainly by the time of the church leader Athanasius in the fourth century, the number of books had long been fixed. He set out the books of the New Testament just as we know them and added:

> These are the fountains of salvation, that whoever thirsts may be satisfied by the eloquence which is in them. In them alone is set forth the doctrine of piety. Let no one add to them, nor take anything from them.[3]

Today, however, there are attempts to undermine the clear witness of history; a host of publications, from the novel to the (supposedly) academic challenge the long-held convictions of Christians and the clear evidence of the past. Dan Brown in *The Da Vinci Code* claimed, "More than eighty gospels were considered for the New Testament, and yet only relatively few were chosen for inclusion—Matthew, Mark, Luke and John among them."[4] Richard Dawkins, professor of popular science at Oxford, England, has made similar comments.[5]

So, what is the evidence for our collection of 66 books? How certain can we be that these are the correct books to make up our Bible—no more and no less?

The canon of the Old Testament

The Jews had a clearly defined body of Scriptures that collectively could be summarized as the Torah, or Law. This was fixed early in the life of Israel, and there was no doubt as to which books belonged and which did not. They did not order them in the same way as our Old Testament, but the same books were there. *The Law* was the first five books, known as the Pentateuch, which means "five rolls"—referring to the parchment scrolls on which they were normally written. *The Prophets* consisted of the Former Prophets (unusually for us these included Joshua, Judges, Samuel, and Kings) and the Latter Prophets (Isaiah, Jeremiah which included Lamentations, and the 12 smaller prophetic books). *The Writings* gathered up the rest. The total amounted generally to 24 books because many books, such as 1 and 2 Samuel and Ezra and Nehemiah, were counted as one.

When was the canon of the Old Testament settled? The simple response is that if we accept the reasonable position that each of the books was written at the time of its history—the first five at the time of Moses, the historical records close to the period they record, the psalms of David during his lifetime, and the prophets written at the time they were given—then the successive stages of acceptance into the canon of Scripture is not hard to fix. Certainly, the Jews generally held this view.

There is a lot of internal evidence that the books of the Old Testament were written close to the time they record. For example, in 2 Chronicles 10:19, we have a record from the time of Rehoboam that "Israel has been in rebellion against the house of David to this day." Clearly, therefore, that must have been recorded prior to 722 BC, when the Assyrians finally crushed Israel and the cream of the population was taken away into captivity—or at the very latest before 586 BC, when Jerusalem suffered the same fate. We know also that the words of the prophets were written down in their own lifetime; Jeremiah had a secretary called Baruch for this very purpose (Jeremiah 36:4).

Josephus, the Jewish historian writing around AD 90, clearly stated in his defense of Judaism that, unlike the Greeks, the Jews did not have many books:

> For we have not an innumerable multitude of books among us, disagreeing from and contradicting one another [as the Greeks have] but only twenty-two books, which contain the records of all the past times; which are justly believed to be divine.[6]

The Council of Jamnia

Between AD 90 and 100, a group of Jewish scholars met at Jamnia in Israel to consider matters relating to the Hebrew Scriptures. It has been suggested that the canon of the Jewish Scriptures was agreed here; the reality is that there is no contemporary record of the deliberations at Jamnia and our knowledge is therefore left to the comments of later rabbis. The idea that there was no clear canon of the Hebrew Scriptures before AD 100 is not only in conflict with the testimony of Josephus and others, but has also been seriously challenged more recently. It is now generally accepted that Jamnia was not a council nor did it pronounce on the Jewish canon; rather it was an assembly that examined and discussed the Hebrew Scriptures. The purpose of Jamnia was not to decide which books should be included among the sacred writings, but to examine those that were already accepted.[7]

The Apocrypha and the Septuagint

There is a cluster of about 14 books, known as the Apocrypha, which were written some time between the close of the Old Testament (after 400 BC) and the beginning of the New. They were never considered as part of the Hebrew Scriptures, and the Jews themselves clearly ruled them out by the confession that there was, throughout that period, no voice of the prophets in the land.[8] They looked forward to a day when "a faithful prophet" should appear.[9]

The Old Testament had been translated into Greek during the third century BC, and this translation is known as the Septuagint, a word meaning *70*, after the supposedly 70 men involved in the translation. It was the Greek Septuagint that the disciples of Jesus frequently used since Greek was the common language of the day.

Whether or not the Septuagint also contained the Apocrypha is impossible to say for certain, since although the earliest copies of

---

the Septuagint available today do include the Apocrypha—placed at the end—these are dated in the fifth century and therefore cannot be relied upon to tell us what was common half a millennium earlier. Significantly, neither Jesus nor any of the apostles ever quoted from the Apocrypha, even though they were obviously using the Greek Septuagint. Josephus was familiar with the Septuagint and made use of it, but he never considered the Apocrypha part of the Scriptures.[10]

The Dead Sea Scrolls

The collection of scrolls that has become available since the discovery of the first texts in 1947 near Wadi Qumran, close by the Dead Sea, does not provide scholars with a definitive list of Old Testament books, but even if it did, it would not necessarily tell us what mainstream orthodox Judaism believed. After all, the Samaritans used only their own version of the Pentateuch, but they did not represent mainstream Judaism.

What can be said for certain, however, is that all Old Testament books are represented among the Qumran collection with the exception of Esther, and they are quoted frequently as Scripture. Nothing else, certainly not the Apocrypha, is given the same status.

In spite of suggestions by critical scholars to the contrary, there is no evidence, not even from the Dead Sea Scrolls, that there were other books contending for a place within the Old Testament canon.

For the Jews, therefore, Scripture as a revelation from God through the prophets ended around 450 BC with the close of the book of Malachi. This was the Bible of Jesus and His disciples, and it was precisely the same in content as our Old Testament.

The New Testament scholar John Wenham concludes: "There is no reason to doubt that the canon of the Old Testament is substantially Ezra's canon, just as the Pentateuch was substantially Moses' canon."[11]

Jesus, His disciples, and the early church leaders

For their part, the Christian community both in the days of Jesus and in the centuries following had no doubt that there was a body of books that made up the records of the old covenant. Since there are literally hundreds of direct quotations or clear allusions to Old Testament passages by Jesus and the apostles, it is evident what the early Christians thought of the Hebrew Scriptures. The New Testament writers rarely quote from other books and never with the same authority. The Apocrypha is entirely absent in their writing.

While it is true that some of the early church leaders quoted from the Apocrypha—though very rarely compared to their use of the Old Testament books—there is no evidence that they recognized these books as equal to the Old Testament.[12]

The conviction that there was a canon of old covenant books that could not be added to or subtracted from doubtless led the early Christians to expect the same divine order for the story of Jesus, the record of the early church, and the letters of the apostles.

The canon of the New Testament

The earliest available list of New Testament books is known as the Muratorian Canon and is dated around AD 150. It includes the four Gospels, Acts, thirteen letters of Paul, Jude, two (perhaps all three) letters of John, and the Revelation of John. It claims that these were accepted by the "universal church." This leaves out 1 and 2 Peter, James, and Hebrews. However, 1 Peter was widely accepted by this time and may be an oversight by the compiler (or the later copyist). No other books are present except the Wisdom of Solomon, but this must be an error since that book belongs in the Apocrypha and no one ever added it to the New Testament!

By AD 240, Origen from Alexandria was using all our 27 books as "Scripture," and no others, and referred to them as the "New Testament."[13] He believed them to be "inspired by the Spirit."[14] But it was not until AD 367 that Athanasius, also from Alexandria, provided us with an actual *list* of New Testament books identical with ours.[15]

However, long before we have that list, the evidence shows that the 27 books, and only those, were widely accepted as Scripture.

Why did it take so long?

The New Testament was not all neatly printed and bound by the Macedonian Publishing Company at Thessalonica shortly after Paul's death and sent out by the pallet load into all the bookstores and kiosks of the Roman Empire. Here are six reasons why it took time for the books of the New Testament to be gathered together.

1. The originals were scattered across the whole empire. The Roman Empire reached from Britain to Persia, and it would have taken time for any church even to learn about all the letters Paul had written, let alone gather copies of them.

2. No scroll could easily contain more than one or two books. It would be impossible to fit more than one Gospel onto a scroll, and even when codices (books) were used, the entire New Testament would be extremely bulky and very expensive to produce. It was therefore far more convenient for New Testament books to be copied singly or in small groups.

3. The first-century Christians expected the immediate return of Christ. Because of this, they didn't plan for the long-term future of the Church.

4. No one church or leader bossed all the others. There were

strong and respected leaders among the churches, but Christianity had no supreme bishop who dictated to all the others which books belonged to the canon and which did not.

5. The early leaders assumed the authority of the Gospels and the apostles. It was considered sufficient to quote the Gospels and apostles, since their authority was self-evident. They did not need a list—inconvenient for us, but not significant for them.

6. Only when the heretics attacked the truth was the importance of a canon appreciated. It was not until the mid-second century that the Gnostics and others began writing their own *pseudepigrapha* (false writing); this prompted orthodox leaders to become alert to the need for stating which books had been recognized across the churches.

In the light of all this, the marvel is not how long it took before the majority of the churches acknowledged a completed canon of the New Testament, but how soon after their writing each book was accepted as authoritative.

Facts about the New Testament canon

• There were only ever the four Gospels used by the churches for the life and ministry of Jesus. Other pseudo-gospels were written but these were immediately rejected by the churches across the empire as spurious.

• The Acts of the Apostles and 13 letters of Paul were all accepted without question or hesitation from the earliest records.

• Apart from James, Jude, 2 and 3 John, 2 Peter, Hebrews, and Revelation, all other New Testament books had been universally accepted by AD 180. Only a few churches hesitated over these seven.

• Well before the close of the first century, Clement of Rome quoted from or referred to more than half the New Testament and claimed that Paul wrote "in the Spirit" and that his letters were "Scriptures."

- Polycarp, who was martyred in AD 155, quoted from 16 NT books and referred to them as "Sacred Scriptures."

- Irenaeus of Lyons, one of the most able defenders of the faith, around AD 180 quoted over 1,000 passages from all but four or five New Testament books, and called them "the Scriptures" given by the Holy Spirit.

- Tertullian of Carthage, around AD 200, was the first serious expositor and used almost all the NT books. They were equated with the Old Testament, and he referred to "the majesty of our Scriptures." He clearly possessed a canon almost, if not wholly, identical to ours.

- By AD 240, Origen of Alexandria was using all our 27 books, and only those, as Scripture alongside the Old Testament books.

And these are just examples of many of the church leaders at this time.

What made a book "Scripture"?

At first, the churches had no need to define what made a book special and equal to the Old Testament Scriptures. If the letter came from Paul or Peter, that was sufficient. However, it was not long before others began writing additional letters and gospels either to fill the gaps or to propagate their own ideas. Some tests became necessary, and during the first 200 years, five tests were used at various times.

1. Apostolic—does it come from an apostle?

The first Christians asked, "Was it written by an apostle or under the direction of an apostle?" They expected this just as the Jews had expected theirs to be underwritten by the prophets. Paul was insistent that his readers should be reassured that the letters they received actually came from his pen (e.g., 2 Thessalonians 3:17).

2. Authentic—does it have the ring of truth?

The authoritative voice of the prophets, "This is what the Lord says," is matched by the apostles' claim to write not the words of men but the words of God (1 Thessalonians 2:13). It was the internal witness of the texts themselves that was strong evidence of canonicity.

3. Ancient—has it been used from the earliest times?

Most of the false writings were rejected simply because they were too new to be apostolic. Early in the fourth century, Athanasius listed the New Testament canon as we know it today and claimed that these were the books "received by us through tradition as belonging to the Canon."[16]

4. Accepted—are most of the churches using it?

Since, as we have seen, it took time for letters to circulate among the churches, it is all the more significant that 23 of the 27 books were almost universally accepted well before the middle of the second century.

When tradition carries the weight of the overwhelming majority of churches throughout the widely scattered Christian communities across the vast Roman Empire, with no one church controlling the beliefs of all the others, it has to be taken seriously.

5. Accurate—does it conform to the orthodox teaching of the churches?

There was widespread agreement among the churches across the empire as to the content of the Christian message. Irenaeus asked the question whether a particular writing was consistent with what the churches taught.[17]

This is what ruled out so much of the heretical material immediately.

Providence

Our final appeal is not to man, not even to the early church leaders, but to God, who by His Holy Spirit has put His seal upon the New Testament. By their spiritual content and by the claim of their human writers, the 27 books of our New Testament form part of the "God breathed" Scripture. It is perfectly correct to allow this divine intervention to guard the process by which eventually all the canonical books—and no others—were accepted. The idea of the final canon being an accident, and that any number of books could have ended up in the Bible, ignores the evident unity and provable accuracy of the whole collection of 27 books.

Bruce Metzger expressed it well: "There are, in fact, no historical data that prevent one from acquiescing in the conviction held by the Church Universal that, despite the very human factors . . . in the production, preservation, and collection of the books of the New Testament, the whole process can also be rightly characterized as the result of divine overruling."[18]

A belief in the authority and inerrancy of Scripture is bound to a belief in the divine preservation of the canon. The God who "breathed out" (2 Timothy 3:16) His word into the minds of the writers ensured that those books, and no others, formed part of the completed canon of the Bible.

1. For a more full discussion of the inspiration of the Bible, see Brian Edwards, *Nothing But the Truth* (Darlington, UK: Evangelical Press, 2006), pp.116–143. In this, the following definition can be found: "The Holy Spirit moved men to write. He allowed them to use their own style, culture, gifts and character, to use the results of their own study and research, to write of their own experiences and to express what was in their mind. At the same time, the Holy Spirit did not allow error to influence their writings; he overruled in the expression of thought and in the choice of words. Thus they recorded accurately all that God wanted them to say and exactly how he wanted them to say it, in their own character, style and language."

2. Clement of Alexandria, *The Miscellanies* bk. vol.15. He comments, "The ecclesiastical rule (canon) is the concord and harmony of the Law and the Prophets." B.F. Westcott, referring to Origen's commentary on Matthew 28, wrote: "No one should use for the proof of doctrine books not included among the canonized Scriptures." (*The Canon of the New Testament During the First Four Centuries* (Cambridge: Macmillan & Co.,1855), p. 548).

3. From the Festal Epistle of Athanasius XXXIX. Translated in *Nicene and Post-Nicene Fathers*, vol. IV., pp. 551–552.

4. Dan Brown, *The Da Vinci Code* (London: Bantam Press, 2003), p. 231.

5. Richard Dawkins, *The God Delusion* (London: Bantam Press, 2006), p. 237.

6. Josephus, *Against Apion*, trans. William Whiston (London: Ward, Lock & Co.), bk. 1, ch. 8. His 22 books consisted of exactly the same as our 39 for the reasons given in the text.

7. This is a widespread view. See for example R. Beckwith, *The Old Testament Canon of the New Testament Church* (London: SPCK, 1985), p. 276. Also, A. Bentzen, *Introduction to the Old Testament*, vol. 1 (Copenhagen: G.E.C. Gad, 1948), p. 31; Bruce Metzger, *The Canon of the New Testament* (Oxford: Oxford University Press, 1987), p. 110; John Wenham, *Christ and the Bible* (London: Tyndale Press, 1972), pp.138–139.

8. The Apocrypha. 1 Maccabees 9:27 at the time of revolt against Syrian occupation in the mid second century BC by Judas Maccabeas: "There was a great affliction in Israel, the like whereof was not since the time that a prophet was not seen among them."

9. The Apocrypha. 1 Maccabees 14:41.

10. It should be noted that the Roman Catholic and Eastern Orthodox churches do accept some of the Apocryphal books as Scripture because they support, for example, praying for the dead.

11. John Wenham, *Christ and the Bible* (London: Tyndale Press, 1972), p.134.

12. This is a point made firmly by John Wenham in *Christ and the Bible*, pp. 146–147.

13. *Origen De Principiis (Concerning Principles)*, pref. 4. He used the title "New Testament" six times in *De Principiis*.

14. *Origen De Principiis*, pref. 4, ch. 3:1.

15. From the Festal Epistle of Athanasius XXXIX. Translated in *Nicene and Post-Nicene Fathers,* vol. IV. pp. 551–552. This is what he wrote: "As the heretics are quoting apocryphal writings, an evil which was rife even as early as when St. Luke wrote his gospel, therefore I have thought good to set forth clearly what books have been received by us through tradition as belonging to the Canon, and which we believe to be divine. [Then follows the books of the Old Testament with the unusual addition of the Epistle of Baruch.] Of the New Testament these are the books . . . [then follows the 27 books of our New Testament, and no more]. These are the fountains of salvation, that whoever thirsts, may be satisfied by the eloquence which is in them. In them alone is set forth the doctrine of piety. Let no one add to them, nor take anything from them."

16. Athanasius, *Festal Epistle* XXXIX.

17. Irenaeus, *Against Heresies*, bk. III, ch. 3:3. "This is most abundant proof that there is one and the same vivifying faith, which has been preserved in the Church from the apostles until now, and handed down in truth."

18. Metzger, *The Canon of the New Testament*, p. 285.

Brian H. Edwards was pastor of an evangelical church in a southwest London suburb for twenty-nine years, and then president of the Fellowship of Independent Evangelical Churches from 1995–1998. He is the author of sixteen books, and continues a ministry of writing and itinerant preaching and lecturing.

Is the Bible Enough?

by Paul F. Taylor

For so many people today, it would appear that the Bible is not enough.

This is the case even (or perhaps especially) among people who have not actually read it. Witness the current popularity of those who would add extra books to the canon of Scripture. Or witness the claims that certain ancient documents are supposedly *more reliable* than the books of the Bible but were kept out of the canon because of petty jealousies.

The last few years have seen the publication of books such as *Holy Grail, Holy Blood*; *The Da Vinci Code*; and *The Gospel of Judas*. What such works proclaim, along with myriad TV documentaries, is that our Bible is suspect, allegedly having been compiled some three centuries after Christ by the winners of an intense theological/political debate. Are such claims true? Are there really other books that should be viewed as Scripture?

Other chapters in this book lay to rest the myth that the Bible was compiled three centuries after Christ. It is the purpose of this chapter to show that the books that allegedly "didn't quite make it" are not inspired and have no merit compared with the books that are part of the canon of Scripture.

Canon

We have become quite used to the word *canon* these days. The word is frequently used of a body of literature. For example, one can refer to the complete works of Shakespeare as the *Shakespearian* canon. More bizarrely, I recently read a discussion about whether certain novels about *Doctor Who* could be considered to be part of the *Doctor Who* canon. Strangely, this last usage was closer to the correct use of the word *canon*, as applied to Scripture. The argument went that the novels introduced concepts and ideas that were later contradicted or not found to be in harmony with events reported in the recent revised TV series. Presumably, the writer of the article felt that these *Doctor Who* novels were not following an accepted rule or pattern.

The word *canon*, in the context of literature, comes from a Greek word meaning "rule." We see the word used in Galatians 6:16.

> And as many as walk according to this rule, peace and mercy be upon them, and upon the Israel of God.

The Greek word for the word *rule* is *kanon*, from which we derive the word *canon*. The word is not referring to a law, but rather a way of doing things—a pattern of behavior. In the context of biblical literature, the word implies that the Bible is self-authenticating—that it is not merely complete, but that it is also internally self-consistent.

It is possible to interpret different passages of the Bible as if they contradict each other, but if one approaches the Bible acknowledging that it is internally self-consistent, then the alleged discrepancies all easily disappear. That is why the apostle Peter describes the people who twist Scripture in this way as "untaught and unstable" (2 Peter 3:16). The extrabiblical writings—and the so-called missing gospels—do not pass the test of self-consistency with the rest of Scripture and are therefore easy to dismiss as not being part of the consistent whole pattern of the Bible—the *canon*.

Apocrypha

The existence in the English language of names such as Toby (from Tobit) and Judith testify to the fact that the so-called Apocrypha was once influential in English society. The word *apocrypha* comes from the Greek word meaning "hidden." However, it popularly refers to a group of books considered by the Roman Catholic Church as part of the Old Testament.

Traditionally, Protestant churches have dismissed the apocryphal books. For example, Article VI of the Church of England's Thirty-Nine Articles lists first the canonical books of the Old Testament, and then lists the apocryphal books prefaced with this warning:

> And the other Books (as Hierome saith) the Church doth read for example of life and instruction of manners; but yet doth it not apply them to establish any doctrine.

The Hierome referred to in the Articles is Jerome. Jerome lived c. 347 to c. 420. He translated the Bible into Latin—the well-known *Vulgate* or common version. Originally, he used the Septuagint as the source of his Old Testament translation. The Septuagint (usually abbreviated to LXX) is a translation of the Old Testament into Greek. Many LXX manuscripts contain the apocryphal books. However, Jerome later revised the Vulgate, going back to Hebrew manuscripts for the Old Testament. It was at this point that he expressed dissatisfaction with the apocrypha, making the comment the Church of England used in its Articles above.

This illustrates that it was not merely a Protestant Reformation decision to remove the Apocrypha. In fact, the Apocrypha was never originally part of the OT canon and was added later. Interestingly, the apocryphal books themselves do not actually claim to be canonical. For example, in 1 Maccabees 9:27, the writer states: "So there was a great affliction in Israel, unlike anything since the time *a prophet had ceased to be seen among them*" (emphasis mine). Moreover, New Testament writers do not quote from apocryphal books, even though they are prepared to quote from other extrabiblical books (e.g., Paul quoted from Greek poets in Acts 17, and Jude quoted from the *Book of Enoch*).

The apocryphal books fail the internal self-consistency test. For example, 2 Maccabees 12:42 contains this exhortation to pray for the dead.

> And they turned to prayer, beseeching that the sin which had been committed [by the dead] might be wholly blotted out (Revised Oxford Apocrypha).

This sentiment is contrary to what is found in the rest of Scripture, both Old and New Testaments, such as Deuteronomy 18:11 and Hebrews 9:27. Similarly, inconsistencies and inaccuracies can be found between other apocryphal books and the correct canon of Scripture.

Da Vinci decoded

Much of the modern preoccupation with extrabiblical writings has come from the publication of Dan Brown's novel *The Da Vinci Code*, and the earlier "serious" treatise on the subject, *Holy Blood, Holy Grail* by Richard Leigh and Michael Baigent. These, and other sensational books and TV documentaries, tend to focus on opposing biblical truth by stating the following:

- Jesus did not die on the cross.

- Jesus married, or had a close and sexual relationship with, Mary Magdalene.

- Mary Magdalene was the leader of the new "church," but misogynist disciples usurped her position.

- These "truths" have been kept secret from the general public over the centuries and are known only to special initiates.

The "initiates" who have this secret knowledge are reputed to be found in many of the traditional "secret" organizations, such as Freemasons or the Knights Templar. At the heart of the so-called secret knowledge are the various doctrines and practices collectively known as *Gnosticism*. Before one even notes the way in which Gnosticism diverges from biblical truth, it is worth reflecting that the Bible makes claim that it should be understood mostly by plain reading. Gnostics, on the other hand, always have codes or secret knowledge required to interpret what God has said. Perhaps it was Gnostics that the apostle Paul had in mind when he warned Timothy thus:

> O Timothy! Guard what was committed to your trust, avoiding the profane and idle babblings and contradictions of what is falsely called knowledge—by professing it some have strayed concerning the faith. Grace be with you. Amen (1 Timothy 6:20–21).

The Greek word for *knowledge* in this passage is *gnosis*, meaning *knowledge*. In the Authorized Version, the word is translated as *science*. Certainly, Paul's criticism of the requirement for special knowledge is pertinent even if he didn't actually have the people we know as Gnostics in mind.

In his book *The Missing Gospels*, Darrell Bock shows that the documents and people labeled as *Gnostic* in fact hold to quite a wide variety of views and doctrines. There are, however, some common traits:

> An essential aspect of Gnosticism was its view of deity, namely, the distinction between and relationship of the transcendent God to the Creator God. This is important because this view of God produced the orthodox reaction against those texts.[1]

Bock observes five characteristics by which Gnostic writings differ from the Bible:

1. Dualism. Gnostics see a distinction between the transcendent God and the Creator God.

2. Cosmogony. This leads to a different view of the universe. Gnostics see an eternal battle between good and evil and do not view God as necessarily being more powerful than the devil.

3. Soteriology. Gnosticism's mode of salvation is by gaining the higher levels of secret knowledge.

4. Eschatology. In common with their view that matter is suspect, Gnostics are not usually looking forward to a bodily resurrection.

5. Cult. Gnostic groups perform various rituals. One of those described in *The Da Vinci Code* involved one of the characters taking part in a naked dance in the forest.

Bock goes on to place the rise of Gnosticism as clearly later than the writing of biblical texts, though there may be reference to Gnostic principles in the passage quoted above. Bock shows Gnosticism to be an unbiblical aberration, rather than being able to live up to the claim that it is the correct teaching of Christ—and that all the other scholars down the centuries have it wrong.

Are these books really Scripture?

Brian Edwards has produced a useful little summary of Gnostic ideas as presented in *The Da Vinci Code*.[2] Some of his thoughts are further summarized in the following.

The *Gospel of Thomas* does not contain a life story. Instead, it is a collection of 114 alleged sayings of Jesus. Some of these are contrary to the rest of Scripture. Not one serious scholar believes that the document was written by the apostle Thomas.

The *Gospel of Philip* contains a lot of Gnostic teaching. Some of the teachings are obscure, in a mystical kind of way, such as:

Light and darkness, life and death, right and left, are brothers of one another. They are inseparable. Because of this neither are the good good, nor evil evil, nor is life life nor death death.

Other teachings are aberrant, such as the idea that God made a mistake in creation:

For he who created it wanted to create it imperishable and immortal. He fell short of attaining his desire.

The teaching given here is that the world is imperfect because God made a mistake. The Bible makes clear that God did indeed make the world perfect, but it is imperfect today because of our sin. In other words, by this teaching, Gnosticism is seeking to remove the responsibility from the human race and hand it to God.

The *Gospel of Mary* purports to be by Mary Magdalene. It certainly attempts to boost her position. It is an article of faith in Dan Brown's novel that Mary Magdalene was actually Jesus's chosen successor and wife—and mother of his child.

> Peter said to Mary, "Sister we know that the Savior loved you more than the rest of women. Tell us the words of the Savior which you remember, which you know, but we do not, nor have we heard them." Mary answered and said, "What is hidden from you I will proclaim to you."

The legends put forward in the books by Brown and Baigent and Leigh are not new. The legend is that, after the crucifixion, Mary fled, as she was pregnant with Jesus's son. She eventually arrived in what is today called France. The Merovingian dynasty claimed to be descended from her, as did Joan of Arc, as did the Stuart dynasty in Scotland and England. They claim that the Holy Grail was actually Mary's womb, and now represents the so-called holy bloodline of descendants of Jesus.

One thinks immediately of Isaiah 53, where the prophet makes clear that the Messiah, the Suffering Servant, will have no descendants.

> He was taken from prison and from judgment, and who will declare His generation? For He was cut off from the land of the living; for the transgressions of My people He was stricken (Isaiah 53:8).

The only people who can really have any claim of "descent" from Jesus are those of us who are saved by repentance and faith in Him.

> When You make His soul an offering for sin, He shall see His seed, He shall prolong His days, and the pleasure of the Lord shall prosper in His hand. He shall see the labor of His soul, and be satisfied. By His knowledge My righteous Servant shall justify many, for He shall bear their iniquities. (Isaiah 53:10–11)

The concept of a married Jesus runs counter to the whole theme of the Bible. Passages in both Old and New Testaments compare our relationship with the Savior as individuals, but more specifically as the Church to a marriage. See, for example, Song of Songs, Psalm 45, and Revelation 19. If Jesus had a real, earthly wife, then this analogy would be inappropriate.

In the *Gospel of Barnabas*, it is claimed that Judas took on the appearance of Jesus and was mistakenly crucified in Jesus's place. The gospel also claims that Jesus told His mother and disciples that He had not been crucified.

It is noteworthy that the *Gospel of Barnabas* claims that the Messiah was to be descended, not from Isaac, but from Ishmael. The document is therefore much quoted by Muslims wanting to prove Islam to be the true faith. It has since been found that it was written in medieval times long after Christ.[3]

The *Gospel of Judas*, an extraordinary document written by Gnostics, claims that Jesus taught one message to 11 of His disciples, but a special, true, secret message to Judas. As part of the secret plan, Jesus persuaded Judas to "betray" Him, thus taking on the highest service for Jesus. This rehabilitation of Judas is remarkable, but as with other Gnostic writings, the authenticity of authorship is dubious, plus it still suffers from being entirely contrary to what is taught in actual biblical books.

Other publications

The *Book of Enoch* falls into a different category from the pseudepigraphal or apocryphal works listed above. Although it is an intertestamental book, it is not part of the official Apocrypha. No books from the official Apocrypha are quoted in the New Testament, but there is a quote from the *Book of Enoch*; Jude quotes a prophecy of Enoch (see verses 14–15), taken from Enoch 1:9. It should be noted that the inclusion of such a quotation in a canonical work does not qualify the rest of the *Book of Enoch* to be part of the canon of Scripture. A similar example is that Paul quotes Greek poets in his address at Mars Hill in Athens (Acts 17). Clearly, the inclusion of this particular prophecy of Enoch proves this individual prophecy to be inspired, but it is not possible therefore to assume inspiration of any of the rest of the book.

A similar claim of authority is sometimes made for the *Book of Jasher*. This book is mentioned in the Bible twice. It is referred to in Joshua 10:13 and again in 2 Samuel 1:18. The title literally means "the book of the upright one." This book is, however, lost, and this loss would itself seem to underline that it is not an inspired, canonical book. Once again, the mention in the Bible of extrabiblical literature does not in itself add any authenticity to that literature. Numerous manuscripts have been published claiming to be the actual *Book of Jasher*. The most well known of these was published by the Church of Jesus Christ of Latter Day Saints. Another example of their literature is discussed below.

The popular name for the Latter Day Saints' Church is *Mormonism*. This name derives from their main "holy" book, the *Book of Mormon*. Many Christians have written detailed criticism of this work, so this paragraph can do no more than scratch the surface. Suffice it to say that there are many reasons why the *Book of Mormon* cannot be accepted as genuine Scripture. The teenaged "prophet" Joseph Smith supposedly translated it from gold plates. These plates have conveniently vanished. It is remarkable, therefore, that some passages of this book quote word for word not just from the Bible, but from a specific translation of the Bible—the KJV. If the book were genuinely inspired, one might expect it to include the same material. But for the wording to be identical to a specific English translation, when the OT was in Hebrew and the *Book of Mormon* supposedly in some other language, is beyond coincidence—for example, compare Isaiah 53:5 from the KJV with Mosiah 14:5. Even the (noninspired) verse divisions are identical, proving that the *Book of Mormon*, far from translating God's words from gold plates, is, in fact, just made up while using direct copies from books such as the KJV Bible.

The Watchtower Bible and Tract Society, or Jehovah's Witnesses, have published a number of magazines (*Watchtower, Awake*, etc.) and books, without which, they claim, it is impossible to interpret the Bible correctly. Although they claim to believe only the Bible, in practice, their religion has added to God's words. Not only that, but it has changed God's Word to suit its own ends. For example, their *New World Translation* of the Bible famously renders John 1:1 as, "In the beginning was the Word, and the Word was with God and the Word was *a god*" (emphasis mine). This use of the term *a god* is in contradiction to all accepted translations, and indeed is contrary to the rabbinical concept of the *Mamre* (or Word of God), to which John, under inspiration, was alluding. As with Mormon literature above, there is a great deal more to be said on the subject of Watchtower literature.

Conclusion

From Edwards and Bock we have seen that the Gnostic documents are of dubious authenticity, not having been written by the authors claimed for them. Secondly, we have seen that their teaching fails the internal self-consistency test, as the documents contain teaching that is counter to what is taught in the accepted canon of Scripture.

The Bible is under severe attack in today's world. Most of that attack seems to be centered on the Book of Genesis, but this is not an exclusive attack. What better way to undermine our belief in Scripture than to produce extra books, outside of the Bible, claiming that their omission from the Bible was merely due to fourth-century politics.

Neither the Old Testament Apocrypha nor the so-called missing gospels have any right to be treated as Scripture. Their authorship is dubious, their quotability negligible, and their agreement with the rest of Scripture nonexistent. Moreover, the argument about the listing of the canon not occurring until the third or fourth centuries is fallacious. As early as AD 90, verses from New Testament books were being quoted and referred to as Scripture.

The reader can be sure to have confidence in God's Word. It is all true—all 66 books of the accepted canon. For those who would disbelieve parts of the Bible, there is a warning. For those who would like to study all these other possible ways to God, the same warning applies:

> Every word of God is pure; He is a shield to those who put their trust in Him. Do not add to His words, lest He rebuke you, and you be found a liar (Proverbs 30:5–6).

1. Darrell Bock, *The Missing Gospels* (Nashville, TN: Thomas Nelson, 2006), p. 21.

2. Brian H. Edwards, *Da Vinci: A Broken Code* (Leominster, UK: Day One Publications, 2006).

3. Answering Islam, "The Gospel of Barnabas," www.answering-islam.org/Nehls/Answer/barnabas.html.

Paul F. Taylor graduated with his BSc in chemistry from Nottingham University and his masters in science education from Cardiff University. Paul taught science for 17 years in a state school and is now a proficient writer and speaker for Answers in Genesis–UK.

Isn't the Bible Full of Contradictions?

by Paul F. Taylor

A Christian talk radio show in America frequently broadcasts an advertisement for a product. In this ad, a young lady explains her take on Scripture: "The Bible was written a long time ago, and there wasn't a lot of knowledge back then. I think that if you read between the lines, it kinda contradicts itself." The show's host replies, "Oh no, it doesn't!" but nevertheless her view is a common view among many people.

Some years ago, I was participating in an Internet forum discussion on this topic. Another participant kept insisting that the Bible couldn't be true because it contradicts itself. Eventually, I challenged him to post two or three contradictions, and I would answer them for him. He posted over 40 alleged contradictions.

I spent four hours researching each one of those points and then posted a reply to every single one. Within 30 seconds, he had replied that my answers were nonsense. Obviously, he had not read my answers. He was not interested in the answers. He already had an *a priori* commitment to believing the Bible was false and full of contradictions. It is instructive to note that after a quick Google search, I discovered that his list of supposed Bible contradictions had been copied and pasted directly from a website.

This anecdote shows that, for many people, the belief that the Bible contains contradictions and inaccuracies is an excuse for not believing. Many such people have not actually read the Bible for themselves. Still fewer have analyzed any of the alleged contradictions. It has been my experience that, after a little research, all the alleged contradictions and inaccuracies are explainable.

If you, the reader, are prepared to look at these answers with an open mind, then you will discover that the excuse of supposed inaccuracies does not hold water. If, however, you have already convinced yourself that such an old book as the Bible just has to contain errors, then you may as well skip this chapter. Like my Internet forum opponent, nothing (apart from the work of the Holy Spirit) is going to convince you that the Bible is 100 percent reliable—especially not the facts!

On giants' shoulders

In attempting to explain some of the Bible's alleged errors, I am standing on the shoulders of giants. I will not be able to address every alleged error for reason of space; others have done the job before me. In my opinion, chief among these is John W. Haley, who wrote the definitive work on the subject, *Alleged Discrepancies of the Bible*.[1] Haley tackles a comprehensive list of alleged discrepancies under the headings "doctrinal," "ethical," and "historical." This chapter uses a similar thematic approach because it will be possible to examine only a representative sample of alleged discrepancies. Readers are referred to Haley's work for a more exhaustive analysis of the subject.

Law of noncontradiction (A ≠ non-A)

One of our own presuppositions could be labeled as the "law of noncontradiction." This stems directly from the belief that the Bible is the inspired, inerrant, and authoritative word of God. Although the 66 books of the Bible were written by diverse human authors in differing styles over a long period of time, it is our contention that the Bible really has only one author—God. The law of noncontradiction has been defined by theologian James Montgomery Boice as follows: "If the Bible is truly from God, and if God is a God of truth (as He is), then . . . if two parts seem to be in opposition or in contradiction to each other, our interpretation of one or both of these parts must be in error."[2] Wayne Grudem makes the same point thus:

> When the psalmist says, "The sum of your word is truth; and every one of your righteous ordinances endures for ever" (Ps 119:160), he implies that God's words are not only true individually but also viewed together as a whole. Viewed collectively, their "sum" is also "truth." Ultimately, there is no internal contradiction either in Scripture or in God's own thoughts.[3]

Boice proceeds to describe two people who are attempting to understand why we no longer perform animal sacrifices. One sees the issue as consistent with the evolution of religion. Another emphasizes the biblical concept of Jesus's ultimate and perfect fulfillment and completion of the sacrificial system. Boice says:

> The only difference is that one approaches Scripture looking for contradiction and development. The other approaches Scripture as if God has written it and therefore looks for unity, allowing one passage to throw light on another.[4]

Our presupposition that the Bible will not contain error is justified by the Bible itself. In Titus 1:2, Paul refers to God "who cannot lie," and the writer to the Hebrews, in 6:17–18, shows that by His counsel and His oath "it is impossible for God to lie." However, if a Bible student is determined to find error in the Bible, he will find it. It is a self-fulfilling prophecy. Yet, the error is not really there.

Inerrancy only for original manuscripts

Historical evangelical statements of faith claim inerrancy for the Scriptures for the original manuscripts. Apparently, this is a problem for some and leads to claims of inconsistency. The argument goes that there have been many translators and copyists since the Bible times and that these translators and copyists must have made errors. Therefore, it is said, we cannot trust current translations of the Bible to be accurate. Boice asks if an appeal to an inerrant Bible is meaningless.

> It would be if two things were true: (1) if the number of apparent errors remained constant as one moved back through the copies toward the original writing and (2) if believers in infallibility appealed to an original that differed substantially from the best manuscript copies in existence. But neither is the case.[5]

In fact, recent discoveries of biblical texts show that the Bible is substantially the same as when it was written. What few discrepancies might still remain are due to mistranslations or mis-

understandings. These issues are all known to biblical scholars and are easily explained.

Presuppositional discrepancies

A number of alleged Bible discrepancies could be described as *presuppositional discrepancies*. What I mean by the term is that there are a number of alleged discrepancies that are only discrepancies because of the presuppositions of the one making the allegations. Many such alleged discrepancies involve scientific argument and are covered in detail in other literature, including elsewhere in this book. Such discrepancies disappear immediately if the reader decides to interpret them in the light of a belief in the truth of the Bible.

The Bible indicates that the world is only 6,000 years old and was created in six days, but science has proved that the earth is millions of years old.

This sort of alleged discrepancy is very common. The supposed inaccuracy of the early chapters of Genesis is very often used as a reason to state that the whole Bible is not true. Many articles on the Answers in Genesis website (www.answersingenesis. org) and in *Answers* magazine tackle such issues, so it is not relevant to repeat the arguments again here. Readers are referred to the chapter "Did Jesus Say He Created in Six Literal Days?" in the *New Answers Book 1*[6] or to my detailed analysis in the *Six Days of Genesis*.[7]

A belief in the truth of Scripture from the very first verse is a reasonable and rational position to take. Once that point is understood, many of these pseudoscientific objections to Scripture fade away.

Let us briefly comment on another such presuppositional discrepancy.

Genesis 6–8 suggest that the whole world was once covered by water. There is no evidence for this.

Detailed answers to this allegation can, once again, be found in much of our literature. For example, see the relevant chapter in the *The New Answers Book*.[8]

It cannot be emphasized too strongly that creationists and evolutionists do not have different scientific evidence. We have the same scientific evidence; the *interpretation* of this evidence is different.

Thus, if one starts from the assumption that the fossil record was laid down over millions of years before human beings evolved, then the fossils do not provide evidence for the Flood. However, if one starts with the presupposition that the Bible's account is true, then we see the fossil record itself as evidence for a worldwide flood and there is no evidence of millions of years! As Ken Ham has often said, "If there really was a worldwide flood, what would you expect to see? Billions of dead things, buried in rock layers laid down by water all over the earth." This is exactly what we see.

Incorrect context

Strongly related to the presuppositional discrepancies are the supposed errors caused by taking verses out of context. For example, a passage in the Bible states, "There is no God." However, the meaning of the phrase is very clear when we read the context: "The fool has said in his heart, 'There is no God.'" (Psalm 14:1). The words "There is no God" are consequently found on the lips of someone the Bible describes as a *fool*.[9]

This discrepancy might seem trivial, but there are more sophisticated examples of the same problem. These often arise by comparing two separate passages, which are referring to slightly different circumstances. For example, consider the following:

Ecclesiastes says that we are upright, while Psalms says that we are sinners.

The verses to which this statement alludes are these:

God made man upright (Ecclesiastes 7:29).

Behold, I was brought forth in iniquity (Psalm 51:5).

Looking at the contexts of both verses removes the discrepancy. In Ecclesiastes 7:29, the writer is talking about Adam and Eve, stating that we were *originally* created upright. In Psalm 51, David is speaking of his personal situation as a sinner, especially in the light of his sinful adultery with Bathsheba and his causing the death of Uriah. Thus, there is no contradiction between these passages.

Translational errors

A common allegation against the Bible is that it is likely to have been mistranslated. When one actually analyzes possible mistranslations, however, it is found that there are actually very few real mistranslations. All of these have been studied and documented and can be found in Haley's book. As we have a number of good English translations today, it is often helpful to compare a couple of these. Once this comparison has been made, many of the so-called translational errors disappear.

There are two creation accounts: Genesis 1 and 2 give different accounts. In chapter 1, man and woman are created at the same time after the creation of the animals. In chapter 2, the animals are created after people.

This apparent contradiction is best illustrated by looking at Genesis 2:19.

Out of the ground the Lord God formed every beast of the field and every bird of the air, and brought them to Adam to see what he would call them (NKJV).

The language appears to suggest that God made the animals after making Adam and then He brought the animals to Adam. However, in Genesis 1, we have an account of God creating animals *and then* creating men and women.

The difficulty with Genesis 2:19 lies with the use of the word *formed*. The same style is read in the KJV.

> And out of the ground the Lord God formed every beast of the field, and every fowl of the air; and brought them unto Adam to see what he would call them.

The NIV has a subtly different rendition.

> Now the Lord God had formed out of the ground all the beasts of the field and all the birds of the air. He brought them to the man to see what he would name them.

The NIV suggests a different way of viewing the first two chapters of Genesis. Genesis 2 does not suggest a chronology. That is why the NIV suggests using the style "the Lord God *had formed* out of the ground all the beasts of the fields." Therefore, the animals being brought to Adam had already been made and were not being brought to him immediately after their creation. Interestingly, Tyndale agrees with the NIV—and Tyndale's translation predates the KJV.

> The Lord God had made of the earth all manner of beasts of the field and all manner fowls of the air.

Tyndale and the NIV are correct on this verse because the verb in the sentence can be translated as *pluperfect* rather than *perfect*. The pluperfect tense can be considered as the past of the past—that is to say, in a narration set in the past, the event to which the narration refers is already further in the past. Once the pluperfect is taken into account, the perceived contradiction completely disappears.

In the Book of Leviticus, bats are described as birds.

The passage to which the allegation refers is Leviticus 11:13–20.

13 And these you shall regard as an abomination among the birds; they shall not be eaten, they are an abomination: the eagle, the vulture, the buzzard,

14 the kite, and the falcon after its kind;

15 every raven after its kind,

16 the ostrich, the short-eared owl, the sea gull, and the hawk after its kind;

17 the little owl, the fisher owl, and the screech owl;

18 the white owl, the jackdaw, and the carrion vulture;

19 the stork, the heron after its kind, the hoopoe, and the bat.

20 All flying insects that creep on all fours shall be an abomination to you (NKJV).

13 And these are they which ye shall have in abomination among the **fowls**; they shall not be eaten, they are an abomination: the eagle, and the ossifrage, and the osprey,

14 And the vulture, and the kite after his kind;

15 Every raven after his kind;

16 And the owl, and the night hawk, and the cuckow, and

the hawk after his kind,

17 And the little owl, and the cormorant, and the great owl,

18 And the swan, and the pelican, and the gier eagle,

19 And the stork, the heron after her kind, and the lapwing, and the bat.

20 All **fowls** that creep, going upon all four, shall be an abomination unto you (KJV).

Bible critics point out that, in their view, the writer of Leviticus is ignorant. He must have thought bats were birds, whereas we now classify them as mammals. Many Bible critics might also go on to discuss the supposed evolutionary origin of bats and birds.

A look at the KJV sheds some light on what the passage actually means. The KJV uses the word *fowls* instead of *birds*. Today, we would not see a significant difference, but notice that the KJV also describes insects as *fowls* in verse 20. The actual Hebrew word is *owph* (Strong's 05775). Although *bird* is usually a good translation of *owph*, it more accurately means *has a wing*. It is therefore completely in order for the word to be used of birds, flying insects, and bats. It could presumably also be used of the pteranodons and other flying reptiles.

This translation of *owph* is supported by noting its use in Genesis 1:20.

> Then God said, "Let the waters abound with an abundance of living creatures, and let birds fly above the earth across the face of the firmament of the heavens" (NKJV).

How could the young Samuel have been sleeping in the Temple when the Temple was not built until much later?

There are two allegations referred to in 1 Samuel 3:3. The verse is quoted below from the KJV, the NIV, and the NKJV.

And ere the lamp of God went out in the temple of the Lord, where the ark of God was, and Samuel was laid down to sleep (KJV).

The lamp of God had not yet gone out, and Samuel was lying down in the temple of the Lord, where the ark of God was (NIV).

And before the lamp of God went out in the tabernacle of the Lord where the ark of God was, and while Samuel was lying down (NKJV).

The translation used by the NKJV gives a clue as to where the first misunderstanding comes from. The Hebrew word is *hēkāl*. This word is used of the temple, but the word is literally a large building or edifice. Commentators[10] have suggested that before the building of the temple the word was often applied to the sacred tabernacle. Therefore, it is perfectly possible for Samuel to have been asleep in this tabernacle. This alleged discrepancy is not so much a mistranslation as a misunderstanding.

The other alleged discrepancy with this verse is that Samuel was sleeping in the sacred portion of this tabernacle, the holy of holies, where the ark of God was. The NKJV gets it correct by pointing out that light went out where the holy of holies was while Samuel was lying down, not that he was lying down in this very holy place. This shows the difficulty of translating Hebrew into English when not careful. This brings us to our next section, where we find alleged discrepancies due to use of language.

Use of language

Some alleged discrepancies occur because of the way that language has changed. It is interesting that while Hebrew has changed very little over the centuries, English is a language undergoing constant major change. The study of how English has altered is fascinating, though outside the scope of this chapter. As an aside, we can easily see how different strands of English have developed in different ways. The best example of this is the divergence between British and American English—a source of tremendous scope for misunderstanding, one-upmanship, and humor (or is it humour?).

Many of the biblical misunderstandings caused by change of language are found in the KJV, which was first translated in 1611. The English language has changed much since 1611, on both sides of the Atlantic. For example, we know that few people today refer to each other as *thee* and *thou,* except some of the older generation in the counties of Lancashire and Yorkshire in Northern England. The KJV uses this terminology to address God, and we can mistakenly think that this is a term of respect. In fact, the use of *thou* is much more specific. It is used to refer to a close friend or relative. In a society that uses the word *thou*, it would never be used in reference to someone to whom one was being especially polite. For example, in his youth my Lancastrian father would refer to his school friends as *thee* but to his teacher as *you*. Therefore, to refer to God as *thou*, while certainly not being disrespectful, implies a degree of intimacy usually associated with families or close friends.

Genesis 1 must contain a gap, because God commanded people to "replenish" the earth. You cannot replenish something, unless it was once previously full.

Genesis 1:28 contains the following command: "Be fruitful, and multiply, and replenish the earth, and subdue it" (KJV). Most other translations use the word *fill* rather than *replenish*. In fact, the Tyndale Bible, which predates the KJV, uses the word *fill*. So did the translators of the KJV get it wrong?

On the contrary. The word *replenish* was a very suitable word to choose in 1611 because at that time the word meant *to fill*

Replenish

Then—1611 | **Today**

Replenish | REPLENISH

Hebrew word in Genesis 1:28 means

Meant to FILL | **Means to REFILL** | **TO FILL, TO FILL UP**

completely, refuting any alleged gap. It therefore carries a slightly stronger emphasis than simply the word *fill*, and the Hebrew word has this emphasis. The word *replenish* did not imply doing something again as many words beginning with *re* do. Its etymology is common with the word *replete*, which still today carries no connotation of a repeated action. However, over the centuries the meaning of *replenish* has altered, so that if we now, for example, suggest replenishing the stock cupboard, we are suggesting that we refill a cupboard, which is now less full than it once was.

There are many other examples of misunderstandings caused by these changes in the English language. None of these misunderstandings were caused by errors on the part of the KJV translators. In fact, they chose the best English words at the time. The problems are caused simply because of the way that English has changed.

Another example of this is to ask why the Psalmist seems to be trying to prevent God from doing something in Psalm 88.

> But unto thee have I cried, O Lord; and in the morning shall my prayer *prevent* thee (Psalm 88:13, KJV, emphasis mine).

The NKJV renders the same verse as follows:

> But to You I have cried out, O Lord, And in the morning my prayer *comes before* You (Psalm 88:13, NKJV, emphasis mine).

Which translation is correct? The answer is that they both are. In 1611, the word *prevent* meant *to come before.* Compare the French verb *venir* (to come) with *prevenir* (to come before). However, in the following centuries, the word *prevent* has altered its meaning in English.

Some problems with use of language exist because of the sort of idioms used in the original languages, which would have been familiar to the original readers but sometimes pass us by. For example:

Moses says insects have four legs, whereas we know they have six.

I have come across this alleged discrepancy frequently. I sometimes wonder if those using this allegation have really thought it through. Do they honestly believe that Moses was so thick that he couldn't count the legs on an insect correctly?

The passage concerned is Leviticus 11:20–23.

> All flying insects that creep on all fours shall be an abomination to you. Yet these you may eat of every flying insect that creeps on all fours: those which have jointed legs above their feet with which to leap on the earth. These you may eat: the locust after its kind, the destroying locust after its kind, the cricket after its kind, and the grasshopper after its kind (NKJV).

In fact, we use the phrase *on all fours* in a similar manner to Hebrew. The phrase is colloquial. It is referring to the actions of the creature (i.e., walking around) rather than being a complete inventory of the creature's feet. Also, when the Bible is referring to locusts and similar insects, it is actually being very precise. Such insects do indeed have four legs with which to "creep" and another two legs with which to "leap," which Moses points out (*those which have jointed legs above their feet with which to leap*). Once again, we find that the allegation of biblical discrepancy does not show up under the light of common sense.

If Jesus was to be in the grave three days and nights, how do we fit those between Good Friday and Easter Sunday?

There are several solutions to this problem. Some have suggested that a special Sabbath might have occurred, so that Jesus was actually crucified on a Thursday. However, a solution, which seems to me to be more convincing, is that Jesus was indeed crucified on a Friday but that the Jewish method of counting days was not the same as ours.

In Esther 4:16, we find Esther exhorting Mordecai to persuade the Jews to fast. "Neither eat nor drink for three days, night or day" (NKJV). This was clearly in preparation for her highly risky attempt to see the king. Yet just two verses later, in Esther 5:1, we read: "Now it happened on the third day that Esther put on her royal robes and stood in the inner court of the king's palace."

If three days and nights were counted in the same way as we count them today, then Esther could not have seen the king until the fourth day. This is completely analogous to the situation with Jesus's crucifixion and resurrection.

> For as Jonah was three days and three nights in the belly of the great fish, so will the Son of Man be three days and three nights in the heart of the earth (Matthew 12:40, NKJV).

> Now after the Sabbath, as the first day of the week began to dawn, Mary Magdalene and the other Mary came to see the tomb (Matthew 28:1, NKJV).

Then, as they were afraid and bowed their faces to the earth, they said to them, "Why do you seek the living among the dead? He is not here, but is risen! Remember how He spoke to you when He was still in Galilee, saying, 'The Son of Man must be delivered into the hands of sinful men, and be crucified, and the third day rise again'" (Luke 24:5–7, NKJV).

If the three days and nights were counted the way we count them, then Jesus would have to rise on the fourth day. But, by comparing these passages, we can see that in the minds of people in Bible times, "the third day" *is equivalent to* "after three days."

In fact, the way they counted was this: part of a day would be counted as one day. Jesus died on Good Friday; that was day one. In total, day one includes the day and the previous night, even though Jesus died in the day. So, although only part of Friday was left, that was the first day and night to be counted. Saturday was day two. Jesus rose in the morning of the Sunday. That was day three. Thus, by Jewish counting, we have three days and nights, yet Jesus rose on the third day.[11]

It should not be a surprise to us that a different culture used a different method of counting days. As soon as we adopt this method of counting, all the supposed biblical problems with counting the days disappear.

Copyist error

It does not undermine our belief in the inerrancy of Scripture to suppose that there may be a small number of copyist errors. With a little logical analysis, this sort of error is not too difficult to spot.

> There must be an error in Luke 3:36. The genealogy gives an extra Cainan not found in similar genealogies, such as Genesis 11:12.

Expositor Dr. John Gill gives ample reasons why this was a copyist error.[12]

Gill says:

> This Cainan is not mentioned by Moses in Genesis 11:12 nor has he ever appeared in any Hebrew copy of the Old Testament, nor in the Samaritan version, nor in the Targum; nor is he mentioned by Josephus, nor in 1 Chronicles 1:24 where the genealogy is repeated; nor is it in Beza's most ancient Greek copy of Luke: it indeed stands in the present copies of the Septuagint, but was not originally there; and therefore could not be taken by Luke from thence, but seems to be owing to some early negligent transcriber of Luke's Gospel, and since put into the Septuagint to give it authority: I say "early," because it is in many Greek copies, and in the Vulgate Latin, and all the Oriental versions, even in the Syriac, the oldest of them; but ought not to stand neither in the text, nor in any version: for certain it is, there never was such a Cainan, the son of Arphaxad, for Salah was his son; and with him the next words should be connected.

If the first Cainan was not present in the original, then the Greek may have read in a manner similar to the following. Remember that NT Greek had no spaces, punctuation, or lower case letters.

ΤΟΘΣΑΡΟΘΨΤΟΘΡΑΓΑΘΤΟΘΦΑΛΕΓΤΟΘΕΒΕΡΤΟΘΣΑΛΑ
ΤΟΘΑΡΦΑΧΑΔΤΟΘΣΗΜΤΟΘΝ6ΕΤΟΘΛΑΜΕΨ
ΤΟΘΜΑΥΟΘΣΑΛΑΤΟΘΕΝ6ΨΤΟΘΙΑΡΕΔΤΟΘΜΑΛΕΛΕΗΛ'''
ΤΟΘΚΑΙΝΑΝ
ΤΟΘΕΝ6ΣΤΟΘΣΗΥΤΟΘΑΛΑΜΤΟΘΥΕΟΘ

If an early copyist glanced at the third line, while copying the first line, it is conceivable that the phrase ΤΟΘΚΑΙΝΑΝ (son of Cainan) may have been copied there.

ΤΟΘΣΑΡΟΘΨΤΟΘΡΑΓΑΘΤΟΘΦΑΛΕΓΤΟΘΕΒΕΡ‴
ΤΟΘΣΑΛΑΤΟΘΚΑΙΝΑΝ
ΤΟΘΑΡΦΑΧΑΔΤΟΘΣΗΜΤΟΘΝ6ΕΤΟΘΛΑΜΕΨ
ΤΟΘΜΑΥΟΘΣΑΛΑΤΟΘΕΝ6ΨΤΟΘΙΑΡΕΔΤΟΘΜΑΛΕΛΕΗΛ‴
ΤΟΘΚΑΙΝΑΝ
ΤΟΘΕΝ6ΣΤΟΘΣΗΥΤΟΘΑΛΑΜΤΟΘΥΕΟΘ

There is some circumstantial evidence for this theory. The Septuagint (LXX) is a Greek translation of the Old Testament said to be translated by about 72 rabbis. Early copies of LXX do not have the extra Cainan in Genesis 11, but later copies postdating Luke's gospel do have the extra Cainan.

It might seem odd to suggest that there could be a copyist error in our translations of the Bible. What is even more remarkable to me, however, is that such possible copyist errors are so extremely rare. Paradoxically, the possible existence of such an error merely reinforces how God has preserved His Word through the centuries.

Conclusion

This chapter has discussed only some of the many alleged Bible contradictions and discrepancies. However, the methods of disposing of the supposed discrepancies used here can also be used on other alleged errors. There is one matter on which the reader should be very confident—the supposed Bible errors are well known to Bible scholars and have all been addressed and found not to be errors after all. In every case, there is a logical explanation for the supposed error. The Bible is a book we can trust—no, more than that—it is the *only* book we can fully trust.

1.   John W. Haley, *Alleged Discrepancies of the Bible* (Grand Rapids, MI: Baker, 1988). The book was originally published in 1874.

2.   James M. Boice, *Foundations of the Christian Faith* (Downers Grove, IL: InterVarsity Press, 1986), p. 91.

3.   Wayne Grudem, *Systematic Theology* (Grand Rapids, MI: Zondervan, 1994), p. 35.

4.   Boice, *Foundations of the Christian Faith*, p. 93.

5.   Boice, *Foundations of the Christian Faith*, p. 75.

6.   Ken Ham, ed., *The New Answers Book 1* (Green Forest, AR: Master Books, 2007).

7.   Paul F. Taylor, *The Six Days of Genesis*, (Green Forest, AR: Master Books, 2007).

8.   Ham, "Was There Really a Noah's Ark and Flood?" *The New Answers Book 1*.

9.   Unless otherwise stated, Bible passages quoted in this chapter are from the New King James Version (NKJV). Other translations are indicated by standard letters, such as KJV (King James Version), NIV (New International Version), and Tyndale (William Tyndale's translation).

10. See, for example, Haley, *Alleged Discrepancies of the Bible*, p. 396.

11. Christian Apologetics and Research Ministry, "How Long Was Jesus Dead in the Tomb?" http://www.carm.org/diff/Matt12_40.htm.

12. Note on Luke 3:36, in: John Gill, D.D., *An Exposition of the Old and New Testament; The Whole Illustrated with Notes, Taken from the Most Ancient Jewish Writings* (London: printed for Mathews and Leigh, 18 Strand, by W. Clowes, Northumberland-Court, 1809). Edited, revised, and updated by Larry Pierce, 1994–1995 for The Word CD-ROM. Available online at http://eword.gospelcom.net/comments/luke/gill/luke3.htm.

Unlocking the Truth of Scripture

by Brian H. Edwards

*T*he Bible is a treasure box. To open the fullness of the treasure within, Christians must use a certain key—hermeneutics, or the rules of interpretation. The correct interpretation of Scripture is almost as important as the doctrine of verbal inspiration itself. There is little value in being able to say, "These are the words of God," if we then interpret them in a way God never intended.

Our goal should be to understand the text as God and the human writers of Scripture intended. To understand correctly any passage of Scripture, Christians must first ask, "What kind of passage is this?"

Different types of passages

Scripture contains a number of different kinds of literature: historical narrative, poetry, parable, epistles (teaching letters), and prophecy. If a passage of Scripture is clearly historical, then we must remember that its purpose is to describe things that actually happened. If a passage is poetic, then we should expect figurative language. Psalm 104, for example, says that God "makes the clouds his chariot" (v. 3), but in light of other Scriptures about God we know that the psalmist here is using a metaphor rather than stating a literal fact.

Prophecy is perhaps the most difficult type of passage to interpret. When faced with prophecy in Scripture, it is important to understand the circumstances behind the prophecy and the relevance to the prophet's own day. The most helpful guide for our understanding of Old Testament prophecy is the way it is explained in the New Testament.

Careful study of Scripture and application of the hermeneutical principles below will enable us to know what kind of literature we are examining and how to interpret it correctly.

What is the context?

1. The biblical context

It is essential to always read the passage around a verse. Who is the writer addressing—believers or nonbelievers, young or old, obedient or disobedient? What topic is being addressed in this passage? What is the unifying theme of this particular book of the Bible? How do the nearby verses help to explain this verse?

2. The historical context

We need to know what was happening in the world at the time the text was written or is describing. Many prophecies make little sense unless we are aware of the threats being made by nations around Israel. The psalms become more vivid when we know, for example, that David wrote some of them while he was being hunted by King Saul in the desert. The historical context is often found in the Bible itself, but a good Bible commentary or Bible encyclopedia will help. These reference books will also help us understand the local customs of the day regarding shepherds, fishing, marriage, clothing, sacrifices, etc., which help explain many passages.

What is the plain meaning?

After we have identified the kind of literature and the context of the passage we are studying, it is important to figure out the grammatical sense and the meaning of the words. We should generally look for the plain meaning, not some mysterious, hidden meaning. It is sound advice that if the literal sense makes good sense, then seek no other sense. Jesus often said, "Have you not read?" He obviously thought that Scripture is basically clear.

Every language has rules of grammar, and we must interpret the Bible according to those rules. For example, many young Christians have difficulty understanding 1 John 3:9 because some translations make it appear that you are not a Christian if you commit a sin. However, the Greek verb is used in a "present continuous" tense, and it means, "No one who is born of God continually commits sin as a way of life."

It is also important to be aware that the same word can have a variety of meanings, depending on its context. In studying the meaning of an individual word, study how the word is used in the passage, in other passages by the same writer, and in the rest of Scripture. (A concordance such as Strong's, a good Bible study computer program, or even a free web-based Bible study tool can be of great help in this regard.)

Like any other book, the Bible uses figures of speech. Recognizing figures of speech is essential to a proper understanding of Scripture. When the Bible uses a simile, metaphor, or figurative language such as hyperbole, it should be interpreted according to the normal usage of such speech. In other words, not everything in the Bible is intended to be taken literally, but the nonliteral figures of speech are plain within context. Genesis 1 is written as literal history, and therefore, it should not be interpreted to be figurative. Context is crucial.

How does this compare with other Scriptures?

Another principle of hermeneutics involves the harmony of Scripture. Because the God of truth inspired the Bible, it contains no contradictions. We must, therefore, compare Scripture with Scripture to make sure that we have interpreted correctly. If our interpretation of one passage contradicts one or more other verses, we have erred; and we need to examine the text more carefully.

How does it apply to me today?

Although application is technically not part of the interpretation process, it is important to note that the Bible was not given to mankind simply for intellectual stimulation, but for life transformation. Jesus indicated that trusting and obeying the Bible leads to more understanding (Matthew 13:10–13).

Beware of the peddlers!

Jesus warned about religious leaders who use the traditions of men to invalidate the Word of God (Mark 7:5–13). Paul warned the Christians at Corinth against those who use the Scriptures to their own ends, often for material gain (2 Corinthians 2:17). Peter warned about people who twist difficult passages to their own destruction (2 Peter 3:16).

Christians need to guard against those who "discover" something new in the Bible. Another danger is those who embellish a Bible story and then treat their additions as if they had God's authority behind them. Christians must, therefore, learn how to "rightly divide" (accurately handle) the Word of God (2 Timothy 2:15).

Conclusion

God wants us to know and apply the treasures of His Word. We should not try to make the Bible say what we want it to mean. Rather, we must carefully apply the common sense principles of hermeneutics to rightly understand w̲   actually said and what He meant. These principles are ea: v, and they are within the reach of everyone who prayer.   are-fully uses them.[1]

Hermeneutics in action: a look at Genesis 1

What type of passage is this?

The writing style of Genesis 1–11 is similar to the style of Genesis 12–50, which Jews have always considered to be a historical account of the beginning of their nation. These chapters do not have the marks of Hebrew poetry (for example, parallelism). And they are not prefaced with "The creation of the world is like . . ." (simile) or clearly identified as a parable (as true parables are). See www.answersingenesis.org/creation/v2/i4/interpretation.asp.

What is the context?

Always read a verse and the passage around it; take care not to be influenced too much by the chapter-and-verse divisions of the Bible. They are not part of the God-breathed Scripture and are often artificial. For example, some claim that Genesis 1 and 2 are contradictory accounts. Notice, however, that the account in Genesis 1 actually continues into Genesis 2 (see verses 1–4). The rest of Genesis 2 is a more detailed account of the creation of man and woman, not a retelling of the entire creation account.[2]

Additionally, the historical accounts found in Genesis 12–50 are merely continuations of the events found in Genesis 1–11. From where came Abraham if his ancestor Adam were merely a myth? See www.answersingenesis.org/Home/Area/wwtl/chapter13.asp.

What is the plain meaning?

Sometimes this question is put a different way: What is the grammatical sense? What do the words mean? Although it has a variety of meanings, the Hebrew word for day (yom) primarily refers to a period of 24 hours, especially when it is used with a number or the phrase "evening and morning" (as it is in Genesis 1). The plain meaning of Genesis is that God created all things in six actual days. The rabbis and church leaders of the past understood that yom referred to actual days, not long periods of time. See www.answersingenesis.org/go/genesis.

What do other Scriptures say?

The best commentary on the Bible is the Bible itself. In this case, Jesus showed that He understood Genesis was true history when He quoted Genesis 1:27 and 2:24 (see Mark 10:6–8). God affirmed that He created in six normal-length days when He wrote the fourth commandment (Exodus 20:11). Paul points out the reality of the First Adam when he compares Adam to Christ (1 Corinthians 15:21–22, 45). Luke traces the ancestry of Jesus back to Adam (Luke 3). It's clear that other Bible writers understood Genesis as a record of actual historical events. See www.answersingenesis.org/articles/nab/did-jesus-say-he-created-in-six-days.

How does this apply to me?

Genesis 1–2 makes it clear that God created humans in His own image, Adam from the dust of the ground and Eve from Adam's rib. We do not share an ancestor with the apes. And God, as our Creator, has given us a standard of right and wrong. We are not free to determine morality on our own. Understanding that the first chapters of Genesis are an accurate account of the past helps us understand that the rest of the Bible can be trusted to tell us the truth in all areas that it touches on. After all, if you can't believe the beginning of the book, why should you believe the end? See www.answersingenesis.org/get-answers/topic/creation-matters.

---

1. Adapted with permission from the book *Nothing But the Truth* by Brian Edwards, published by Evangelical Press.

2. Genesis 2:19 is most appropriately translated as the pluperfect "had formed" (as the NIV has it), which eliminates any perceived contradiction with the order in Genesis 1.

THE BOOK OF MORMON · AN

Holy Bible

Other Religious Writings: Can They Be from God, Too?

by Bodie Hodge

The answer to this question seems too simple: other alleged divine writings are not from God because they are not among the 66 books of the Bible and, in fact, they contradict the Bible.

A presuppositional approach

This is a "presuppositional" approach, which means to presuppose that God exists and that His Word, the Bible, is the truth. This is the starting point or axiom.

God never tried to prove His existence or prove that His Word is superior to other writings. God simply opens the Bible with a statement of His existence and says His Word is flawless (Genesis 1:1; Proverbs 30:5). The Bible bluntly claims to be the truth (Psalm 119:160), and Christ repeated this claim (John 17:17).

In fact, if God had tried to prove that He existed or that His Word was flawless, then any evidence or proof would be greater than God and His Word. But God knows that nothing is greater than His Word, and therefore He doesn't stoop to our carnal desires for such proofs.

The Bible also teaches us to have faith that God exists and that having faith pleases Him (Hebrews 11:6). Accordingly, we are on the right track if we start with God's Word.

So how do we know that other religious writings are not from God?

God will not contradict Himself

In the Bible, we read that God cannot lie (Titus 1:2; Hebrews 6:18). This is significant because it means that God's Word will never have contradictions. Though skeptics have alleged that there are contradictions in the Bible, every such claim has been refuted. This is what we would expect if God's Word were perfect.

Yet the world is filled with other "religious writings" that claim divine origin or that have been treated as equal to or higher than the Bible on matters of truth or guidelines for living. In other words, these writings are treated as a final authority over the Bible.

Any religious writing that claims divine inspiration or authority equal to the Bible can't be from God if it has any contradictions: contradictions with the Bible, contradictions within itself, or contradictions with reality.

Examples of contradictions in religious writings

A religious writing can be tested by comparing what it says to the Bible (1 Thessalonians 5:21). God will never disagree with Himself because God cannot lie (Hebrews 6:18). When the Bible was being written and Paul was preaching to the Bereans (Acts 17:11), he commended them for checking his words against the Scriptures that were already written. If someone claims that a book is of divine origin, then we need to be like the Bereans and test it to confirm whether it disagrees with the 66 books of the Bible. Paul's writings, of course, were Scripture (2 Peter 3:16).

Religious books, such as Islam's Koran, Mormonism's Book of Mormon, and Hinduism's Vedas, contradict the Bible; and so they cannot be Scripture. For example, the Koran in two chapters (Sura 4:171 and 23:91) says God had no son, but the Bible is clear that Jesus is the only begotten Son of God (Matthew 26:63–64).

The Book of Mormon says in Moroni 8:8 that children are not sinners, but the Bible teaches that children are sinful, even from birth (Psalm 51:5). Few would dispute that the Vedas and other writings in Hinduism are starkly different from the Bible.

Also, such religious writings contain contradictions within themselves that are unanswerable without gymnastics of logic. In the Koran, one passage says Jesus will be with God in paradise (Sura 3:45) and another states that He will be in hell for being worshiped by Christians (Sura 21:98).

The Book of Mormon, prior to the 1981 change, says that American Indians will turn white when they convert to Mormonism (2 Nephi 30:6). If such writings were truly from God, such discrepancies couldn't exist.

Since such alleged holy books are not from the perfect God, who are they from? They are from deceived, imperfect mankind. Mankind's fallible reason is not the absolute authority. God and His Word are. Other books may have tremendous value, such as historical insight, but they are not the infallible Word of God.

The Bible warns that false philosophies will be used to turn people from the Bible (Colossians 2:8), so we need to stand firm on the Bible and not be swayed (1 Corinthians 15:58; 2 Thessalonians 2:15).

There are really two options: place our faith in the perfect, all-knowing God who has always been there, or trust in imperfect, fallible mankind and his philosophies. The Bible, God's Holy Word, is superior to all other alleged holy books. God will never be wrong or contradict Himself. So start with the Bible, and build your faith on its teachings so that you please Him.

Quick Comparison

	View of Origins	View of Christ
Bible	God created all things in six 24-hour days, about 6,000 years ago. All creatures, including man, were created after their own kind. Sin, disease, sickness, and death were not part of this creation. They came as a result of the Fall.	Jesus is the only begotten Son of God (God incarnate), who became man to live a perfect life, to be mankind's substitute on the Cross, and to rise from the dead, defeating death.
Islamic Scriptures	The Koran teaches that Allah created all things, but it contradicts itself regarding the number of days. It also teaches that the first man and woman were created in Paradise but were later banished to earth after the fall into sin.	Allah (God) created Jesus and appointed him to be a messenger to the Jewish people. The Koran does teach that Jesus was sinless but He was not God.
Mormon Scriptures	God created man physically after He created the earth. However, we had a pre-earth life, in which we existed as God's "spirit children."	Jesus is the spirit-brother to every man, and even Satan. Jesus is one of an endless number of gods and is a being separate from the Heavenly Father

	Sin and Salvation	**Life after Death**
Bible	Every person has sinned and fallen short of the glory of God. Salvation is by grace through faith in Christ and His redeeming work on the Cross.	Mankind will live forever either in heaven or in hell. The only way for us to get to heaven is through faith in Christ.
Islamic Scriptures	Salvation is possible after adherence to the Koran, as well as performing the five pillars of the Islamic faith. But even then, salvation is not guaranteed.	Allah sends both righteous and unrighteous to hell unless they die in a holy war. But if their good works outweigh their bad, they should be admitted into Paradise. Paradise is only guaranteed to those who die in jihad (holy war).
Mormon Scriptures	Sin was part of God's plan because without it mankind could not progress to become like God, know joy, or have children. Salvation is a combination of faith and works.	Even after death, everyone has an opportunity to respond to the gospel. Heaven has three levels, and those who attain the highest level become gods, ruling and populating their own universe.

Bodie Hodge attended Southern Illinois University at Carbondale (SIUC) and received a BS and MS (in 1996 and 1998 respectively) there in mechanical engineering. His specialty was a subset of mechanical engineering based in advanced materials processing, particularly starting powders.

Bodie conducted research for his master's degree through a grant from Lockheed Martin and developed a New Method of Production of Submicron Titanium Diboride. The new process was able to make titanium diboride cheaper, faster and with higher quality. This technology is essential for some nanotechnologies.

Currently, Bodie is a speaker, writer, and researcher in AiG's Outreach Department.

CHAPTER 1

e beginning God created the
ven and the earth.
d the earth was without form,
id; and darkness *was* upon the
the deep. And the Spirit of
moved upon the face of the wa-

And God said, Let there be
and there was light.
nd God saw the light, that *it was*
and God divided the light
the darkness.
nd God called the light Day,
the darkness he called Night.
the evening and the morning
the first day.

¶ And God said, Let there be a
ament in the midst of the waters
ers, and let it divide the waters
n the waters.
And God made the firmament, and
ded the waters which *were* under
firmament from the waters which
e above the firmament: and it was

And God called the firmament
aven. And the evening and the
orning were the second day.
¶ And God said, Let the waters
der the heaven be gathered to-
ther unto one place, and let the dry
nd appear: and it was so.
0 And God called the dry *land*
arth; and the gathering together
the waters called he Seas: and
od saw that *it was* good.
11 And God said, Let the earth
ring forth grass, the herb yielding
eed, *and* the fruit tree yielding fruit
fter his kind, whose seed *is* in itself,
pon the earth: and it was so.
12 And the earth brought forth
grass, *and* herb yielding seed after his
kind, and the tree yielding fruit, whose
seed *was* in itself, after his kind: and
God saw that *it was* good.
And the evening and the morning
hird day.

the lesser light to rule
made the stars also.
17 And God set ther
ment of the heaven to
the earth,
18 And to rule ov
over the night, and to
from the darkness: an
it was good.
19 And the evening
were the fourth day.
20 And God said
bring forth abund
creature that hath
that may fly abov
open firmament of
21 And God cre
and every living cr
which the waters
dantly, after thei
winged fowl after
saw that *it was* go
22 And God bl
Be fruitful, and
waters in the sea
ply in the earth.
23 And the ev
ing were the fift
24 ¶ And Go
bring forth beast
his kind, cattle
and beast of th
and it was so.
25 And God
earth after his
their kind, and
eth upon the
and God saw
26 ¶ And
man in our i
and let them
fish of the s
the air, and
all the earth
thing that
earth.
27 So Go
image, in t
he him; m
them.
28 And
said unto
multiply.
id, Let there be
heaven

Creation: Where's the Proof?

by Ken Ham

Over the years, many people have challenged me with a question like:

"I've been trying to witness to my friends. They say they don't believe the Bible and aren't interested in the stuff in it. They want real proof that there's a God who created, and then they'll listen to my claims about Christianity. What proof can I give them *without mentioning the Bible* so they'll start to listen to me?"

Briefly, my response is as follows.

Evidence

Creationists and evolutionists, Christians and non-Christians all have the *same* evidence—the same facts. Think about it: we all have the same earth, the same fossil layers, the same animals and plants, the same stars—the facts are all the same.

The difference is in the way we all *interpret* the facts. And why do we interpret facts differently? Because we start with different *presuppositions*. These are things that are assumed to be true, without being able to prove them. These then become the basis for other conclusions. *All* reasoning is based on presuppositions (also called *axioms*). This becomes especially relevant when dealing with past events.

Past and present

We all exist in the present—and the facts all exist in the present. When one is trying to understand how the evidence came about (Where did the animals come from? How did the fossil layers form? etc.), what we are actually trying to do is to connect the past to the present.

However, if we weren't there in the past to observe events, how can we know what happened so we can explain the present? It would be great to have a time machine so we could know for sure about past events.

Christians of course claim they do, in a sense, have a "time machine." They have a book called the Bible which claims to be the Word of God who has always been there, and has revealed to us the major events of the past about which we need to know.

On the basis of these events (Creation, Fall, Flood, Babel, etc.), we have a set of presuppositions to build a way of thinking which enables us to interpret the evidence of the present.

Evolutionists have certain beliefs about the past/present that they presuppose, e.g. no God (or at least none who performed acts of special creation), so they build a different way of thinking to interpret the evidence of the present.

Thus, when Christians and non-Christians argue about the evidence, in reality they are arguing about their *interpretations* based on their *presuppositions*.

That's why the argument often turns into something like:

"Can't you see what I'm talking about?"

"No, I can't. Don't you see how wrong you are?"

"No, I'm not wrong. It's obvious that I'm right."

"No, it's not obvious." And so on.

These two people are arguing about the same evidence, but they are looking at the evidence through different glasses.

It's not until these two people recognize the argument is really about the presuppositions they have to start with, that they will begin to deal with the foundational reasons for their different beliefs. A person will not interpret the evidence differently until they put on a different set of glasses—which means to change one's presuppositions.

I've found that a Christian who understands these things can actually put on the evolutionist's glasses (without accepting the presuppositions as true) and understand how they look at evidence. However, for a number of reasons, including spiritual ones, a non-Christian usually can't put on the Christian's glasses—unless they recognize the presuppositional nature of the battle and are thus beginning to question their own presuppositions.

It is of course sometimes possible that just by presenting "evidence", you can convince a person that a particular scientific argument for creation makes sense "on the facts." But usually, if that person then hears a different *interpretation* of the same evidence that seems better than yours, that person will swing away from your argument, thinking they have found "stronger facts."

However, if you had helped the person to understand this issue of presuppositions, then they will be better able to recognize this for what it is—a different interpretation based on differing presuppositions—i.e. starting beliefs.

As a teacher, I found that whenever I taught the students what I thought were the "facts" for creation, then their other teacher would just re-interpret the facts. The students would then come back to me saying, "Well sir, you need to try again."

However, when I learned to teach my students how we interpret facts, and how interpretations are based on our presuppositions, then when the other teacher tried to reinterpret the facts, the students would challenge the teacher's basic assumptions. Then it wasn't the students who came back to me, but the other teacher! This teacher was upset with me because the students wouldn't accept her interpretation of the evidence and challenged the very basis of her thinking.

What was happening was that I had learned to teach the students *how* to think rather than just *what* to think. What a difference that made to my class! I have been overjoyed to find, sometimes decades later, some of those students telling me how they became active, solid Christians as a result.

Debate terms

If one agrees to a discussion without using the Bible as some people insist, then *they* have set the terms of the debate. In essence these terms are:

1. Facts are neutral. However, there are no such things as "brute facts"; *all* facts are interpreted. Once the Bible is eliminated in the argument, then the Christians' presuppositions are gone, leaving them unable to effectively give an alternate interpretation of the facts. Their opponents then have the upper hand as they still have *their* presuppositions.

2. Truth can/should be determined independent of God. However, the Bible states: "The fear of the Lord is the beginning of wisdom" (Psalm 111:10); "The fear of the Lord is the beginning of knowledge" (Proverbs 1:7). "But the natural man does not receive the things of the Spirit of God, for they are foolishness to him; neither can he know them, because they are spiritually discerned" (1 Corinthians 2:14).

A Christian cannot divorce the spiritual nature of the battle from the battle itself. A non-Christian is *not* neutral. The Bible makes this very clear: "The one who is not with Me is against Me, and the one who does not gather with Me scatters" (Matthew 12:30); "And this is the condemnation, that the Light has come into the world, and men loved darkness rather than the Light, because their deeds were evil" (John 3:19).

Agreeing to such terms of debate also implicitly accepts their proposition that the Bible's account of the universe's history is irrelevant to understanding that history!

Ultimately, God's Word convicts

1 Peter 3:15 and other passages make it clear we are to use every argument we can to convince people of the truth, and 2

Corinthians 10:4–5 says we are to refute error (like Paul did in his ministry to the Gentiles). Nonetheless, we must never forget Hebrews 4:12: "For the word of God is living and powerful and sharper than any two-edged sword, piercing even to the dividing apart of soul and spirit, and of the joints and marrow, and is a discerner of the thoughts and intents of the heart."

Also, Isaiah 55:11: "So shall My word be, which goes out of My mouth; it shall not return to Me void, but it shall accomplish what I please, and it shall certainly do what I sent it to do."

Even though our human arguments may be powerful, ultimately it is God's Word that convicts and opens people to the truth. In all of our arguments, we must not divorce what we are saying from the Word that convicts.

Practical application

When someone tells me they want "proof" or "evidence", not the Bible, my response is as follows:

"You might not believe the Bible but I do. And I believe it gives me the right basis to understand this universe and correctly interpret the facts around me. I'm going to give you some examples of how building my thinking on the Bible explains the world and is not contradicted by science. For instance, the Bible states that God made distinct *kinds* of animals and plants. Let me show you what happens when I build my thinking on this presupposition. I will illustrate how processes such as natural selection, genetic drift, etc. can be explained and interpreted. You will see how the science of genetics makes sense based upon the Bible."

One can of course do this with numerous scientific examples, showing how the issue of sin and judgment, for example, is relevant to geology and fossil evidence. And how the Fall of man, with the subsequent Curse on creation, makes sense of the evidence of harmful mutations, violence, and death.

Once I've explained some of this in detail, I then continue:

"Now let me ask you to defend *your* position concerning these matters. Please show me how *your* way of thinking, based on *your* beliefs, makes sense of the same evidence. And I want you to point out where my science and logic are wrong."

In arguing this way, a Christian is:

Using biblical presuppositions to build a way of thinking to interpret the evidence.

Showing that the Bible and science go hand in hand.

Challenging the presuppositions of the other person (many are unaware they have these).

Forcing the debater to logically defend his position consistent with science and his own presuppositions (many will find that they cannot do this).

Honoring the Word of God that convicts the soul.

Remember, it's no good convincing people to believe in creation, without also leading them to believe and trust in the Creator/Redeemer, Jesus Christ. God honors those who honor His Word. We need to use God-honoring ways of reaching people with the truth of what life is all about.

Naturalism, logic, and reality

Those arguing against creation may not even be conscious of their most basic presupposition, one which excludes God *a priori*, namely naturalism/materialism (everything came from matter, there is no supernatural, no prior creative intelligence). The following two real-life examples highlight some problems with that assumption:

A young man approached me at a seminar and stated, "Well, I still believe in the big bang, and that we arrived here by chance random processes. I don't believe in God." I answered him, "Well, then obviously your brain, and your thought processes, are also the product of randomness. So you don't know whether it evolved the right way, or even what right would mean in that context. Young man, you don't know if you're making correct statements or even whether you're asking me the right questions."

The young man looked at me and blurted out, "What was that book you recommended?" He finally realized that his belief undercut its own foundations —such "reasoning" destroys the very basis for reason.

On another occasion, a man came to me after a seminar and said, "Actually, I'm an atheist. Because I don't believe in God, I don't believe in absolutes, so I recognize that I can't even be sure of reality." I responded, "Then how do you know you're really here making this statement?" "Good point," he replied. "What point?" I asked. The man looked at me, smiled, and said, "Maybe I should go home." I stated, "Maybe it won't be there." "Good point," the man said. "What point?" I replied.

This man certainly got the message. If there is no God, ultimately, philosophically, how can one talk about reality? How can one even rationally believe that there is such a thing as truth, let alone decide what it is?

Ken Ham is President and CEO of Answers in Genesis–USA and the Creation Museum. Ken's bachelor's degree in applied science was awarded by the Queensland Institute of Technology in Australia. He also holds a diploma of education from the University of Queensland. Ken has authored or co-authored many books concerning the authority and accuracy of God's Word and the effects of evolutionary thinking, including *Genesis of a Legacy* and *The Lie: Evolution*. Since moving to America in 1987, Ken has become one of the most in-demand Christian conference speakers in America.

Here I stand, I can do no other

If I profess with the loudest voice
and clearest exposition every portion of
the Word of God except precisely that
little point which the world and the
devil are at that moment attacking, I
am not confessing Christ, however
boldly I may be professing Him.

Where the battle rages there the
loyalty of the soldier is proved; and to
be steady on all the battle front besides
is mere flight and disgrace if he
flinches at that point.

—Martin Luther, correspondence

Is It Time for a New Reformation?

by Ken Ham

Take one look around our world. A need for a new reformation is evident, both for our culture and for the church. We must return to the Bible as our absolute authority.

Whether it's liberalism, evolutionism, Gnosticism, Mormonism, Islam, New Age, moral issues (e.g., abortion and gay marriage), or the age of the earth, these are all ultimately battles over the same issue.

In 2 Corinthians 11:3, the Apostle Paul, under the inspiration of the Holy Spirit, warns us about this ever-present danger: "But I fear, lest somehow, as the serpent deceived Eve by his craftiness, so your minds may be corrupted from the simplicity that is in Christ."

Paul in essence is warning Christians that Satan will continue to use the same method on us as he did on Eve: Satan will try to seduce people away from a simple devotion to Christ and His Word.

To understand this better, we need to go back to Genesis 3:1: "Now the serpent was more crafty than any of the animals the Lord God had made. He said to the woman, 'Did God really say . . . ?'"

From the beginning, the battle was over the authority of the Word of God. The first woman, Eve, followed by her husband, Adam, gave in to the temptation not to take God at His Word. Instead, he relied on his human reason to determine truth.

Because Adam was the head of the human race, his rebellion plunged the entire human race into sin. All his descendants inherited a sin nature that refused to take God at His Word and instead made human reason their supreme authority.

This battle against God's Word has manifested itself in every era of history.

Paul faced skeptics on every side, who questioned the clear proclamation of God's Word. In its early centuries, Christianity fought several challenges to the authority of the Scriptures, including Gnosticism, which taught that man was his own god. Modern issues like the age of dinosaurs or carbon dating are merely new manifestations of age-old attacks on God's Word.

Human reason has replaced God's Word, and compromise has crept into the church. A reformation is needed again to call the church to take God at His Word.

In the sixteenth century, the sale of indulgences by the church, for forgiveness of sin and release from the pains of Purgatory, marked a climax in the elevation of human thinking above God's Word. The monk Martin Luther nailed his 95 theses to the door of the Wittenberg Church, challenging indulgences. This act sparked a debate about the ultimate authority of the Bible above the church, and it essentially began the Reformation.

Others joined this reform movement. The Western world was dramatically changed, as Bibles and tracts were printed on the new presses and thus biblical truths were disseminated widely. In fact, until recent decades, much of the West was still heavily influenced by the Reformation and its call to take God at His Word.

The battle against God's Word never ceased, however, as a series of men and events sought to undo the positive effects of the Reformation. Behind these attacks was an effort to make human reason supreme and steer people away from the authority of the Word of God. It was another manifestation of Genesis 3:1.

In the eighteenth and nineteenth centuries, the attack against the Bible intensified. New speculation about the age of the earth and the evolution of life raised questions about the accuracy of the Bible. The core issues can be seen in the Scopes trial—said to be the most famous and culture-shaping trial in history (other than the trial of Jesus).

The Scopes trial of 1925 was not really about the teaching of evolution, as is commonly believed, but a deliberate ploy by the American Civil Liberties Union to put Christianity as a whole on trial. Even though the prosecution lawyer William Jennings Bryan was a great Christian statesman, he let the Christian faith down by not standing on God's Word concerning the book of Genesis. For example, he was unable to give an answer about Cain's wife, and he allowed the possibility that the earth is millions of years old.

The trial marked a symbolic turning point in Christendom and American society. The world's media reported that Christians were not taking God at His Word (in Genesis), and also that they could not adequately defend it.

The failure of the church to stand on God's Word has brought devastation to countless lives. Just one example is the once-prominent evangelist Charles Templeton. While in seminary, he was taught to believe in an evolutionary timetable, including millions of years, which eventually led him to reject God's Word.

Compromise about biblical authority in Genesis 1–11 has made the church so weak that the Bible no longer impacts the culture as it once did. This has largely occurred because human reason was allowed to invade the church and push aside God's Word.

A new reformation is needed. It's time for a new generation of reformers to stand up and call the church back to trust in God's Word where it is most under attack—the history of Genesis 1–11. Biblical creation ministries, such as the Creation Museum, have already issued the call to turn away from the opinions of fallible mankind and stand firmly on the entire Bible.

It's time that believers made their voices heard, nailing Genesis 1–11 on church doors and secular buildings across the world! We need to take God at His Word and return to the "simplicity that is in Christ." Then we can watch the power of God's Word transform lives and influence the culture.

What is a Biblical Worldview?

by Stacia McKeever

*T*he history as recorded in the Bible has been attacked by our increasingly secular culture. As a result, recent generations have been brought up to see the Bible as a book that contains many interesting stories and religious teaching but has no connection to reality.

This limited viewpoint helps explain why there are so many questions about how the Bible can explain dinosaurs, fossils, death, and suffering and many other topics that relate to our real world.

This chapter will outline the major events of the past (and even the future)—the "7 C's of History"—that are foundational to the Bible's important message and demonstrate how the Bible connects to the real world.

Creation

God created the heavens, the earth and all that is in them in six normal-length days around 6,000 years ago. His completed *creation* was "very good" (Genesis 1:31), and all the original animals (including dinosaurs) and the first two humans (Adam and Eve) ate only plants (Genesis 1:29–30). Life was perfect and not yet affected by the Curse—death, violence, disease, sickness, thorns, and fear had no part in the original creation.

After He was finished creating, God "rested" (or stopped) from His work, although He continues to uphold the creation (Colossians 1:17). His creation of all things in six days and resting on the seventh set a pattern for our week, which He designed for us to follow.

The science of "information theory" confirms that first statement of the Bible, "In the beginning God created . . . ." DNA is the molecule of heredity, part of a staggeringly complex system, more information-dense than that in the most efficient supercomputer. Since the information in our DNA can only come from a source of greater information (or intelligence), there must have been something other than matter in the beginning. This other source must have no limit to its intelligence; in fact, it must be an ultimate source of intelligence from which all things have come. The Bible tells us there is such a source—God. Since God has no beginning and no end and knows all (Psalm 147:5), it makes sense that God is the source of the information we see all around us! This fits with real science, just as we would expect.[1]

In Genesis, God explains that He created things to reproduce after their "kinds." And this is what we observe today: great variation within different "kinds" (e.g., dogs, cats, elephants, etc.), but not one kind changing into another, as molecules-to-man evolution requires.[2]

Corruption

After God completed His perfect creation, He told Adam that he could eat from any tree in the Garden of Eden (Genesis 2:8) except one—the Tree of the Knowledge of Good and Evil. He warned Adam that death would be the punishment for disobedience (Genesis 2:17). Instead of listening to the command of his Creator, Adam chose to rebel, eating the fruit from the tree (Genesis 3:6). Because our holy God must punish sin, He sacrificed animals to make coverings for Adam and Eve, and He sent the first couple from the garden, mercifully denying them access to the Tree of Life so that they would not live forever in their sinful state.

Adam's sin ushered death, sickness, and sorrow into the once-perfect creation (Genesis 3:19; Romans 5:12). God also pronounced a curse on the world, changing it completely (Genesis 3; Romans 8:20–22). As a result, the world that we now live in is merely a decaying remnant—a corruption—of the beautiful, righteous world that Adam and Eve originally called home. We see the results of this corruption all around us in the form of carnivorous animals, mutations, sickness, disease, and death.[3] The good news is that, rather than leave His precious handiwork without hope, God graciously promised to one day send a Redeemer who would buy back His people from the curse of sin (Genesis 3:15).

Catastrophe

As the descendants of Adam and Eve married and filled the earth with offspring, their wickedness was great (Genesis 6:5). God judged their sin by sending a global Flood to destroy all men, animals, creatures that moved along the ground, and birds of the air (Genesis 6:7). Those God chose to enter the Ark—Noah, his family and land-dwelling representatives of the animal kingdom (including dinosaurs)—were saved from the watery *catastrophe*.

There was plenty of room in the huge vessel for tens of thousands of animals—even dinosaurs (the average dinosaur was only the size of a sheep, and Noah didn't have to take fully grown adults of the large dinosaurs). Noah actually needed only about 16,000 animals on the Ark to represent all the distinct kinds of land-dwelling animals.[4]

This earth-covering event has left its mark even today. From the thousands of feet of sedimentary rock found around the world to the "billions of dead things buried in rock layers" (fossils), the Flood reminds us even today that our righteous God cannot—and will not—tolerate sin, while the Ark reminds us that He provides a way of salvation from sin's punishment. The rainbows we experience today remind us of God's promise never again to destroy the earth with water (Genesis 9:13–15). Incidentally, if the Flood were a local event (rather than global in extent), as some claim, then God has repeatedly broken His promise since we continue to experience local flooding even today.[5]

Confusion

After the Flood, God commanded Noah and his family—the only humans left in the world—and the animals to fill the earth (Genesis 8:17). However, the human race once again disobeyed God's command and built a tower, which they hoped would keep them together (Genesis 11:3–4). So, around 100 years after the Flood waters had retreated, God brought a *confusion* (a multiplicity) of languages in place of the common language the people shared, causing them to spread out over the earth. The several different languages created suddenly at Babel (Genesis 10–11) could each subsequently give rise to many more. Languages gradually change; so when a group of people breaks up into several groups that no longer interact, after a few centuries they may each speak a different (but related) language. Today, we have thousands of languages but fewer than twenty language "families."[6]

All the tribes and nations in the world today have descended from these various groups. Despite what you may have been led to believe about our seeming superficial differences, we really are all "one blood" (Acts 17:26)—descendants of Adam and Eve through Noah and his family—and all, therefore, are in need of salvation from sin.

God had created Adam and Eve with the ability to produce children with a variety of different characteristics. This ability was passed on through Noah and his family. As the people scattered, they took with them different amounts of genetic information for certain characteristics—e.g., height, the amount of pigment for hair and skin color (by the way, we all have the same pigment, just more or less of it), and so on.

In fact, the recent Human Genome Project supports this biblical teaching that there is only *one* biological race of humans. As one report says, ". . . it is clear that what is called 'race' . . . reflects just a few continuous traits determined by a tiny fraction of our genes."[7] The basic principles of genetics explain various shades of *one* skin color (not different colors) and how the distinct people groups (e.g., American Indians, Australian Aborigines) came about because of the event at the Tower of Babel. The creation and Flood legends of these peoples, from all around the world, also confirm the Bible's anthropology to be true.

Christ

God's perfect creation was corrupted by Adam when he disobeyed God, ushering sin and death into the world. Because of Adam's disobedience and because we have all sinned personally, we are all deserving of the death penalty and need a Savior (Romans 5:12).

As mentioned before, God did not leave His precious—but corrupted—creation without hope. He promised to one day send Someone who would take away the penalty for sin, which is death (Genesis 3:15; Ezekiel 18:4; Romans 6:23).

God killed at least one animal in the Garden of Eden because of the sin of Adam; subsequently, Adam's descendants sacrificed animals. Such sacrifices could only cover sin—they pointed toward the time when the One whom God would send (Hebrews 9) would make the ultimate sacrifice.

When God gave Moses the Law, people began to see that they could never measure up to God's standard of perfection (Romans 3:20)—if they broke any part of the Law, the result was the same as breaking all of it (James 2:10). They needed Someone to take away their imperfection and present them faultless before God's throne (Romans 5:9; 1 Peter 3:18).

In line with God's purpose and plan for everything, He sent His promised Savior at just the right time (Galatians 4:4). There was a problem, however. All humans are descended from Adam and, therefore, all humans are born with sin. God's chosen One had to be perfect, as well as infinite, to take away the infinite penalty for sin.

God solved this "problem" by sending His Son, Jesus *Christ*—completely human and completely God. Think of it: the Creator of the universe (John 1:1–3, 14) became part of His creation so that He might save His people from their sins!

Jesus fulfilled more than fifty prophecies made about Him centuries before, showing He was the One promised over 4,000 years before by His Father (Genesis 3:15). While He spent over thirty years on Earth, He never once sinned—He did nothing wrong. He healed many people, fed huge crowds, and taught thousands of listeners about their Creator God and how to be reconciled to Him. He even confirmed the truth of Genesis by explaining that marriage is between one man and one woman (Matthew 19:3–6, quoting Genesis 1:27 and Genesis 2:24).

Cross

Jesus is called the "Last Adam" in 1 Corinthians 15:45. While Adam disobeyed God's command not to eat the forbidden fruit,

Jesus fulfilled the Creator's purpose that He die for the sin of the world. The first Adam brought death into the world through his disobedience; the Last Adam brought eternal life with God through His obedience (1 Corinthians 15:21–22).

Because God is perfectly holy, He must punish sin—either the sinner himself or a substitute to bear His wrath. Jesus bore God's wrath for our sin by dying in our place on the *Cross* (Isaiah 53:6). The Lamb of God (John 1:29; Revelation 5:12) was sacrificed once for all (Hebrews 7:27) so that all those who believe in Him will be saved from the ultimate penalty for sin (eternal separation from God) and will live with Him forever.

Jesus Christ, the Creator of all things (John 1:1–3; Colossians 1:15–16), was not defeated by death. He rose three days after He was crucified, showing that He has power over all things, including death, the "last enemy" (1 Corinthians 15:26). As Paul wrote, "O death, where is your sting? O grave, where is your victory? ... But thanks be to God who gives us the victory through our Lord Jesus Christ" (1 Corinthians 15:55, 57).

When we believe in Christ and understand what He has done for us, we are passed from death into life (John 5:24). The names of those who receive Him are written in the Lamb's Book of Life (Revelation 13:8 and Revelation 17:8)—when they die, they will go to be with Him forever (John 3:16).

Just as "science" cannot prove that Jesus rose from the dead, it cannot prove that God created everything in six days. In fact, "science" can't prove any event from history because it is limited in dealings about the past. Historical events are known to be true because of reliable eyewitness accounts. In fact, there are reliable eyewitness accounts that Jesus' tomb was empty after three days and that He later appeared to as many as 500 people at once (1 Corinthians 15:6). Of course, we know that both the Resurrection and creation in six days are true because God, who cannot lie, states in His Word that these things happened.

While the secular history of millions of years isn't true, and evolutionary geology, biology, anthropology, astronomy, etc., do not stand the test of observational science, the Bible's history, from Genesis 1 onward, *is* true; the Bible's geology, biology, anthropology, astronomy, etc., are confirmed by observational science. Therefore, the fact that the Bible's history is true should challenge people to seriously consider the Bible's message of salvation that is based in this history.

Consummation

Death has been around almost as long as humans have. Romans 8 tells us that the whole of creation is suffering because of Adam's sin. As terrible as things are, however, they are not a permanent part of creation.

God, in His great mercy, has promised not to leave His creation in its sinful state. He has promised to do away with the corruption that Adam brought into the world. He has promised to remove, in the future, the curse He placed on His creation (Revelation 22:3) and to make a new heaven and a new Earth (2 Peter 3:13). In this new place there will be no death, crying, or pain (Revelation 21:4).

Those who have repented and believed in what Jesus did for them on the Cross can look forward to the *consummation* of God's kingdom—this new heaven and Earth—knowing they will enjoy God forever in a wonderful place. In the future, God will take away the corruption that was introduced in the Garden of Eden, giving us once again a perfect place to live!

A worldview based on a proper understanding of the history of the world, as revealed in the Bible, is what every Christian needs to combat our society's evolutionary propaganda.

1. For a more in-depth analysis of the complexity of DNA and information theory, see www. AnswersInGenesis.org/infotheory.

2. For more information, see www.AnswersInGenesis.org/liger.

3. For more information, see www.AnswersInGenesis.org/curse.

4. See *Noah's Ark: A Feasibility Study* by John Woodmorappe for a detailed analysis of the capacity of this huge ship to hold all the residents of the Ark.

5. For more information, see www.AnswersInGenesis.org/flood.

6. For more information, see www.AnswersInGenesis.org/linguistics.

7. S. Pääbo, "The Human Genome and Our View of Ourselves," *Science* 291 no. 5507 (2001):1219–1220.

Stacia McKeever graduated summa cum laude in biology and psychology from Clearwater Christian College. She worked full-time for Answers in Genesis-USA from 1997 to 2008. Stacia has written or co-written a number of articles for *Answers* magazine, *Creation* magazine, *Godly Business Woman*, *Teach Kids!*, and the AiG website. She also has written curricula (*Beginnings*, *The Seven C's of History*, *Questions*) and workbooks for elementary-aged children.

Is the Bible Full of Mistakes?

You may have been told that it is. But, have you sincerely considered that claim on your own? If you are like most people, you probably haven't read the Bible, but you are familiar with some of its stories and teachings. You may not realize that all 66 books of the Bible really tell one continuing story, and you are a part of it.

As we look at the Bible, there is one theme that stands out from the beginning to the end—redemption. Now, in order for something to be redeemed, there must be something wrong. The Bible explains that God created the world, including mankind, and He called everything He had created "very good" (Genesis 1:31). God placed Adam and Eve in a garden with only one prohibition—they were not to eat the fruit from the Tree of the Knowledge of Good and Evil (Genesis 2:16, 17). It was not long before this simple command was violated. The penalty for this disobedience is described in Genesis 3 and is referred to as the Fall of man. The entire universe was cursed by God. We live in that fallen world today. If you doubt the world is fallen, look around at all of the examples of death, disease, and suffering—this world is no longer "very good"! As part of this fallen world, each person needs to be redeemed as well.

You might not believe that you are part of the problem, but the Bible makes it clear that every person has sinned against God (Romans 3:23). To help us understand our condition, God has communicated His expectations to us in His Law. God's Law can be summarized by the Ten Commandments (Exodus 20). Can you name any of them? Have you broken any of them? Let's take a little test to see if you have:

1. Have you ever told a lie? (You shall not bear false witness against your neighbor. Exodus 20:16)

2. Have you ever used God's name in a loose way? (You shall not take the name of the LORD your God in vain, for the LORD will not hold him guiltless who takes His name in vain. Exodus 20:7)

3. Have you ever desired something that belongs to someone else? (You shall not covet . . . anything that is your neighbor's. Exodus 20:17)

4. Have you ever looked with lust at someone? (You shall not commit adultery. Exodus 20:14)

If you have broken these commandments, you are, by your own admission, a lying, blaspheming, covetous adulterer. That last one might give you some pause, but Jesus said, "You have heard that it was said to those of old, 'You shall not commit adultery.' But I say to you that whoever looks at a woman to lust for her has already committed adultery with her in his heart" (Matthew 5:27–28).

Maybe you have only broken one of those commands. In James 2:10 we read, "For whoever shall keep the whole law, and yet stumbles in one point, he is guilty of all."

God calls the breaking of His law sin. Because He is an infinite, perfectly holy God, breaking His Law, even in one point, is worthy of an infinite punishment. This is what you need to be redeemed from. You have chosen to rebel against the commands of the God who created you, and God, the Just Judge, must punish that rebellion.

From the very beginning God has offered the hope of redemption from this fallen state that we live in. When He pronounced the Curse in Genesis 3, He also promised that He would provide a Savior (Genesis 3:15). This prophecy was fulfilled by Jesus Christ—God in the flesh.

Jesus stepped down from heaven to take human form, live a perfectly sinless life (not breaking a single command of God), and then die on the Cross receiving the punishment for sin upon Himself. God's wrath against sin was poured out on Christ. Jesus was punished, paying a debt for sin that you and I could never pay. God accepts Jesus's sacrifice on our behalf and our sins can be forgiven so that we do not have to face God's punishment. Jesus was placed in a tomb after He died, but He rose back to life three days later, demonstrating that He has conquered death.

The Bible clearly teaches that all who will repent of their sins and trust in Jesus can be redeemed. To repent, you must admit that you have sinned against God, ask His forgiveness, and then turn from those sins. When you trust in Christ alone for your salvation, God offers eternal life with Him. The Bible speaks of a time when God will redeem the rest of His creation from the Fall, but your personal redemption can happen now.

The Bible makes the claim of truth. Truth, by its very nature, must be exclusive. If you want to be logically consistent, you cannot pick and choose which parts of the Bible you will accept. The Bible itself makes that clear:

> All Scripture is given by inspiration of God, and is profitable for doctrine, for reproof, for correction, for instruction in righteousness, that the man of God may be complete, thoroughly equipped for every good work. 2 Timothy 3:16, 17

> Paul, a bondservant of God and an apostle of Jesus Christ, according to the faith of God's elect and the acknowledgment of the truth which accords with godliness, in hope of eternal life which God, who cannot lie,

promised before time began, but has in due time manifested His word through preaching, which was committed to me according to the commandment of God our Savior. Titus 1:1–3

If the Bible contains the words of God and God cannot lie, those words must be true. Every word of the Bible must be true or every word must be false. You may place yourself in a position of authority over the Bible and reject those claims, but that does not make them false. Where do you stand?